FARM BOY

WORLD

WILLARD INGRAHAM

DEDICATED TO THE MEMORY
OF MY PARENTS

GENA AND LYLE INGRAHAM

Bizy Enterprises, Inc.-Publisher-Gilbert, Arizona

FARM BOY TO SOLDIER
WORLD WARD II

Author: Willard Ingraham

Published by:
Bizy Enterprises, Inc.
929 N. Val Vista Dr.
Suite 107 #191
Gilbert, Arizona 85234

Copyright 2004
ISBN, first print edition 0-9722621-1-3
Publishing date: June 2004

Grateful acknowledgement is made to the editor of The Pekan Newsletter for the information sent for use in this book.

TABLE OF CONTENTS

Acknowledgments
About The Author
Time Line Of Service

Introduction

ACKNOWLEDGEMENT

I would like to give thanks to God and to our Lord Jesus Christ for all the guidance and protection that was given to us in the 526 Armored Infantry Battalion as we were treading in dangerous territory.

Also I give my thanks to God for his daily guidance and blessings realized in my life and the lives of my family. His understanding and help through my life made all things possible.

I am grateful to my wonderful wife, Louise who graciously offered to help me and did all of the typing, insertions and illustrations in the book. She was tremendously helpful in giving me wise pointers along the way.

I also give thanks to my daughter, Mary Ann Hicks who was always willing and able to help me when called upon to do so. As a co-publisher with Milton Hicks it was their publishing business, Bizy Enterprises, Inc. that gave me the platform for putting my work to press.

I thank all of my family for their support and encouragement to me to write this book of memories that covers almost three years of my life while serving in World War II.

It is my desire to encourage the soldiers who served in the 526th to write their own stories in a book as a memento for their own family history. It has been over 60 years ago since we served and time says if we haven't already done so we must write our memories now for those who come after us. I feel that if I can write anyone can put down their own memories in their own words in a book as I did. I pray I have inspired others to put a hand to pen and paper.

ABOUT THE AUTHOR

Willard Ingraham has written his book as he lives his life in ways that are a reflection of his own philosophies. God and his family are the most important elements in his life. He does not consider himself an author yet how he has told his story about his life in the service reveals his ability to write in an interesting manner.

Willard and Louise Ingraham
2004

This is his first book but not the first of the many years he has spent compiling records and stories on genealogy and the history of his family and his wife's family. He believes it is his due to pass down family history so that it is never lost to those who come after. Because he has kept good records through out his life and from the gracious contributions of others he was able to reconstruct a time over 60 years ago.

If he could speak personally to each of the soldiers that served with him he would say as he does to me. "Those years in the service formed the basis of believing anything is possible if one believes in God and we work as a team."

Willard resides in Washington with his wife Louise and continues building on the same principles in life he has always had; God and family first.

FARM BOY TO SOLDIER

BY: Willard Ingraham

This book covers a time in Willard's life from March 1943 to Dec. 29, 1945.

He was inducted in the army at Ft. Douglas, Utah and immediately sent to Ft. Knox, Kentucky for basic training with "A" Company, 2nd Platoon, 526th Armored Infantry Battalion. He moved to Camp Bouse, Az. September 1943 for maneuver training in the desert (Tent City). April 1944 he moved to Staton Island, NY for shipment to Swansea, Wales waiting for D-Day. He was involved in four major battles (Northern France, Ardennes, Rhineland, Central Europe) across France, Luxomber, Belgium and Germany. He also was in the Battle of the Bulge. His battalion was attached to T Force and Counter Intelligence. Corp. Willard was discharged at Ft. Lewis, Washinton, Dec. 29, 1945.

Willard took his headquarters squad, 2nd Platoon A Company 526th Armored Infantry Battalion out searching for some German paratroopers that might have landed in their area.

INTRODUCTION

This book covers a three-year span in the life of Willard Ingraham. His story will begin with his experiences on a farm and continue through his induction and life in the army.

You will follow Willard through basic training at Fort Knox, Kentucky and maneuvers in the hot desert sands of Arizona. These maneuvers included specialized training that prepared him and other soldiers for their assignment in World War II.

The story follows the 526 Armored Infantry Battalion that Willard trained with to the war front. Read what it was like to receive the embarkation notice that sent them on the way to Europe through Fort Hamilton, New York.

Willard describes how attacks on the convoy of ships that carried these soldiers overseas to England took place. Learn how it was that six German submarines were waiting for this US convoy of ships and how the Germans knew the ships would be there.

Know what it was like for these soldiers to be waiting for D-Day while stationed in Wales, Great Britain. Read about the biggest battle of the 526 Armored Infantry Battalion in The Battle Of The Bulge.

Find in what way that the 526 armored infantry battalion was attached to the T force under General Bradley 12th army group.

Willard talks openly for the first time about his life on the front lines. Read of the triumphs and the hardships borne by all the front line soldiers. You will learn what it meant to be a part of a special assignment in a small unit. They lived in foxholes through all the seasons of the year, including winter with snow.

Survival was difficult but Willard's farm boy life and army training helped him through these trying times in his life. You will know what it was like to face the enemy with uncertainty of the outcome. It is an intriguing story told as this young man lived it.

CHAPTER I
STARTING OVER

Herbert Hoover was president of United States in 1929 during the great disastrous depression. It was under his administration that the economic system of America collapsed. The stock market crash created panic that preceded a nationwide depression. Bank closures took place everywhere. There were no federal insurance guarantees that protected people from loss, in effect, shutting people out from retrieving money that was theirs.

In rural America the farmers were unable to borrow money for operating costs due to bank closures. Outstanding loans were called in for lack of none payment. Foreclosures on farms ran rampant.

My parents, Lyle and Gena Ingraham, were farmers and owned a farm out of Woodworth, North Dakota. Our family consisted of my parents and four children. The oldest was Raymond, then Norman, and myself, Willard, and a younger sister Lorraine.

I was five years old when the depression hit but I can remember the hard times. My parents were on a farm where they raised enough food to eat but there was never any extra money for the necessities including money to operate the farm. It was in 1932 when they lost everything.

In the year 1933 Franklin Roosevelt became president of the United States. He established the Works Progress Administration known as the W.P.A. This program gave jobs to many. The Social Security Act passed helping elderly people to survive, as did the Unemployment and Old Age Compensation Act.

With the work programs in place and people back to work money began to flow and families could eat regularly. Hope for a future of families and the United States rose.

THE INGRAHAM FAMILY IN NORTH DAKOTA,   1940
L to R: Willard, Lorraine, Gena, Raymond, Lyle and Norman

My father, at first, would work over 200 miles from home to get a job on the W.P.A. He was lucky to get home once a month. It was rough for everyone but there was enough money that now we were all eating regular meals. If lucky, we children might even get a pair of shoes without holes in the toes.

Dad was a good farmer and found farms to live on as a sharecropper. In the year of 1940 my parents leased a wheat and cattle farm, ten and one-half miles from New Rockford, NorthDakota.

THE NEW ROCKFORD, NORTH DAKOTA FARM 1940
Original painting by: Willard Ingraham

I have fond memories of these times. I had a dog, Tippy, that would go with me wherever I went on the farm. When I brought the cows in for milking they would sometimes be a half-mile away in the pasture. It never mattered how far, Tippy was always with me. The cows would be across the river in the pasture at the further point from the barn. I would wade the river carrying Tippy over with me. She always loved that part of it.

Willard and Tippy

Across the river, in that area was a fox den with about three baby fox.

3

Many times I would sit across the river and watch the little fox

TIPPY

play. The fox got used to me being there after a while and were not frightened by my presence. Although they realized I would not hurt them they were cautious enough to not let me come close enough to pet them or pick them up.

Growing up in North Dakota was not always difficult. Our entertainment was a radio that we would all listen to programs such as, Alley Oop, One Mans Family, Guiding Light, and boxing matches. Major Bow's amateur hour was always a very popular program. It was on this program that many of the contestants would go on to be great entertainers and reach a status of fame.

It may not seem believable for many people in this day and age but in my time T.V. was not thought of yet. In fact, in the early 1940's the radio was just coming into its own as the standard household purchase.

It was in 1941 that there were tremendous changes in the lives of the Ingraham family. In the spring of that year our family survived a devastating tornado that affected more than a dozen farms in our area.

The day of the tornado, our family was sitting in the house relaxing after lunch. On looking out of the window we could see the wind begin to blow the dust across the fields. Dad was watching the weather change very abruptly and he knew that something was about to happen. He had lived through a tornado as a young boy. What he was seeing reminded him of that tornado long ago.

We all watched as the storm increased in intensity. Some objects started to move across the yard pushed by the force of the wind. Suddenly the clouds were boiling like a hot teakettle on a stove. The clouds were dark and rolling in the sky and on the ground our hayrack started moving across the barnyard from the force of the wind.

Dad shouted, "It's a tornado; everyone to the basement." We all made a dash to the basement door except Mom. She thought she must get her purse that was in her bedroom. Raymond and I chased after her to make sure she got to the basement. She retrieved her purse and we were just going down the basement stairs when the full force of the tornado struck. The rest of the family had already made it to the basement.

The house began to shake like it would come apart any minute. Objects from the storm were hitting the house like a bunch of bullets peppering the side of the building. The storm probably only lasted a few minutes but it seemed like a long time and then the wind suddenly stopped and everything got very still except it was raining.

The storm was over and it was safe to go outside to check the damage. Many strange things had happened. The house had holes in the roof. The house had been peppered with small sticks and straw that stuck out of the sides of the house. The barns are built big in North Dakota so that the loft storage

5

BARN AFTER THE TORNADO

space would hold a winter supply of hay to last until spring. We found one 12 inch by 12 inch x 18 foot timber that supported the loft structure of the barn one half mile from home in our wheat field laying all by itself. We had a small amount of hay in the loft of the barn still there intact.

CHICKEN HOUSE NEXT TO THE ROOFLESS BARN

We had a rabbit pen in the loft of the barn with an empty pail that we used to get corn for our pet rabbits sitting on top of the rabbit pen. The pail was still there, unmoved throughout the storm, as the barn was more than half destroyed.

Just the barn was destroyed by the tornado; all the other buildings needed only minor repair. Norman had recently purchased his car so at the time of purchase he had it insured. Of all the three cars standing in the yard, Norman's car was the only car that was damaged and the only car that was covered by insurance.

Now it was time for the cleanup that was done in an orderly fashion. Then crops were planted and we were now looking forward to a bountiful year of good crops.

In the fall, our crops of wheat, corn, and barley all looked very good. Normally, every year, we would cut and bind the wheat into bundles and place in shocks to cure. After they dried they would be sent through a threshing machine to separate the grain from the straw. The year, 1941 was different as something new came to town. It was called a combine.

To combine a crop, the machine would cut the wheat and separate the grain from the straw. As the combine moved down the field it left straw scattered behind. This, of coarse left no time for curing so the crop had to be really ripe when combined. This meant leaving the wheat stand a week longer before harvest could begin.

The combine was brought out to harvest and we watched golden wheat just roll out. I hauled the grain in a truck to the elevator to a little town called Brantford, North Dakota. It was about six miles from our farm.

We got in one day of good harvesting and looked forward to combining the rest of the grain but this was not to happen. That night a hailstorm came in and destroyed all the crops with hail pounding all the grain standing into the ground. It was a total loss of all the rest of the fields of wheat.

By now Dad was getting pretty disgusted with the way the year was progressing. He went to bed one night and by morning he informed the family that he was going to Washington State to buy a farm there.

Three days later Dad was in Washington and had purchased a farm. He wrote a letter to Mom and told her as soon as the transaction was closed he would be back home. In the meantime, he told Mom to tell us boys to get things ready for a sale.

We all got busy and painted some of the farm machinery and lined everything up in a row across the barnyard, ready for the auctioneer and sale day. On October 22, 1941 we had the sale it went very well.

Dad bought a new 1942 Chevrolet ¾ ton pickup then he built a rack on the back. All the remaining personal possessions left after the sale was loaded on the pickup and in the trunks of Raymond's and Norman's cars. The three rigs caravanned on together, Washington bound with all six of us aboard.

The Ingraham family arrived at our new home in the Yakima Valley at Prosser, Washington on a beautiful sunshine day on November 5, 1941. Dad immediately got busy buying new machinery and livestock to get the new farm together. Mom was busy cleaning house and arranging the furniture that was purchased to replace the furniture sold at the sale.

20 ACRE RANCH LYLE INGRAHAM PURCHASE
PROSSER, WASHINGTON, 1941

Ingraham's in Washington, 1941,
Bk L to R. Raymond, Norman, Willard
Fr L to R Gena, Lyle, Lorraine

9

Raymond and Norman went out looking for jobs. Lorraine signed up for school. I was 16 years old and did not sign up to go to high school at that time.

We just got settled in and December 7, 1941 arrived. We all listened to that chilling radio broadcast made by President Roosevelt that Japan had bombed Pearl Harbor.

December 7, 1941: "A day that will live in infamy." The USS *Shaw* exploding during the Japanese attack on Pearl Harbor.

December 8, 1941: President Franklin D. Roosevelt signing the Declaration of War against Japan, one day after the attack on Pearl Harbor.

President Roosevelt not only declared wa[r]
joined England to fight the Germans. Presiden[t]
us that everything would turn out all right and
nothing to fear but fear itself.

All of us boys knew that we would soon be in
uniform. For me, being 16 years old, it would be two years
before I could go.

As you all know, no one knew what TV was at this time
so our only news was the radio. It was the following spring that
I went to work for an elderly couple doing their farm work.
They lived close to home so I purchased a new bicycle to ride
to work.

WILLARD'S 1929 MODEL A FORD COUPE & BICYCLE

It was not long before I found a 1929 Model A Ford
Coupe with a rumble seat. I got it really cheap and fixed it up
to look and run really good. Soon it was summer time and the
fruit packing plants needed help to work with the packing of
fruit. My wages went up about three times the amount I had
gotten doing farm work.

...nt gave the workers all the
...vorking 18 hours a day. I
...s then Mom and Dad saw that
...ght. That was the end of my

...r on Japan but also
...Roosevelt told
...there was

WILLARD'S 1937 CHEVROLET CAR

After working there for a couple of months I decided to
buy a 1937 Chevrolet sedan car. It was green in color and luck
would be with me, the car turned out to be a very good one. I
paid for it in three months. My Uncle Art Steffens rode in my
car several times and remarked what a nice car I had
purchased. He liked the car so well that later when I entered
the Army he purchased it from me.

During the summer months of 1942, my cousin, Arnold
Steffens and I purchased a ten-acre farm with a house, barn,
new chicken house and a grape field. We got a really good
deal on the purchase price so decided, at the time; we would
purchase this ranch, pay for it, and then purchase another farm.

NORMAN WATERING HORSES AFTER WORK IN FIELD

It was now September of 1942 and Norman received his notice to enter the Army in November. Knowing all of us boys would soon be in the service we decided to return to North Dakota for a visit. My cousin, Arnold Steffens, Norman, my brother, and I drove back to North Dakota to see our relatives and friends.

ARNOLD STEFFENS STANDING BY NORMAN'S CAR AND THE THRESHING MACHINE

13

When we got back to New Rockford, North Dakota we discovered that the farmers were feeling the pinch of the Army quotas to the point they needed help to harvest their grain. The farmers talked to all three of us about helping them harvest their grain. We had not planned on helping but finally we all agreed to help them out for a few days. Before leaving to go home to Washington we drove to Jamestown, North Dakota to visit our relatives and grandparents who lived there. Our grandfather, Gunder Johnson, told us as we said our goodbyes that he would never see us again. He was right because he died in 1943.

The November date for Norman's entrance into the army arrived and off he went to Camp Gruber, Oklahoma.

My Uncle, Art Steffens, my cousin Arnold Steffens, my brother Raymond and myself went to work at the Yakima Chief Hop Yards in Mabton, Washington. We helped in their harvest of hops and after that all through the winter we worked clearing apple orchards for more hop fields. In December 1943 and now 18 years old I thought it was about time for me to go serve my country. I went to the Prosser selective service board to volunteer to go into the Air Force. My thinking was that the Air Force would train me to become a pilot.

PVT   NORMAN   INGRAHAM

CHAPTER II

IN THE ARMY NOW

On the 9th of December 1942, I received government notification to go to a local doctor at 9: A.M. on the 14th of

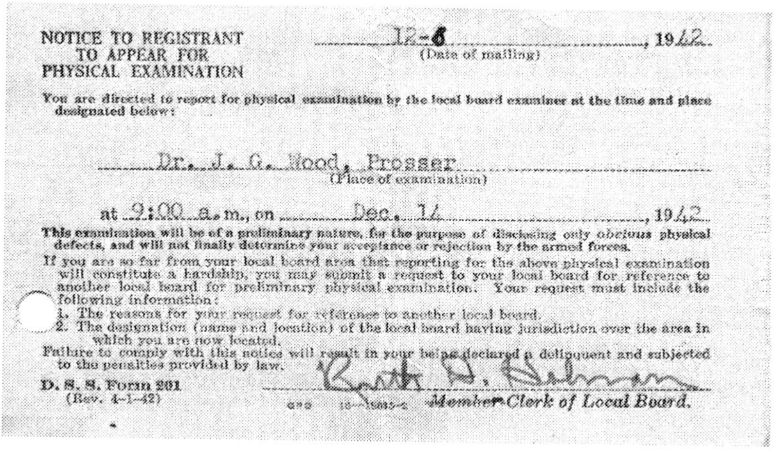

NOTICE TO REGISTRANT TO APPEAR FOR PHYSICAL EXAMINATION

12-6, 1942
(Date of mailing)

You are directed to report for physical examination by the local board examiner at the time and place designated below:

Dr. J. G. Wood, Prosser
(Place of examination)

at 9:00 a.m., on Dec. 14, 1942

This examination will be of a preliminary nature, for the purpose of disclosing only *obvious* physical defects, and will not finally determine your acceptance or rejection by the armed forces.

If you are so far from your local board area that reporting for the above physical examination will constitute a hardship, you may submit a request to your local board for reference to another local board for preliminary physical examination. Your request must include the following information:

1. The reasons for your request for reference to another local board.
2. The designation (name and location) of the local board having jurisdiction over the area in which you are now located.

Failure to comply with this notice will result in your being declared a delinquent and subjected to the penalties provided by law.

D. S. S. Form 201
(Rev. 4-1-42)

Member-Clerk of Local Board.

December to have a physical examination. It was the preliminary to find out if I was physically fit to serve our country. I was found to be physically sound in every way.

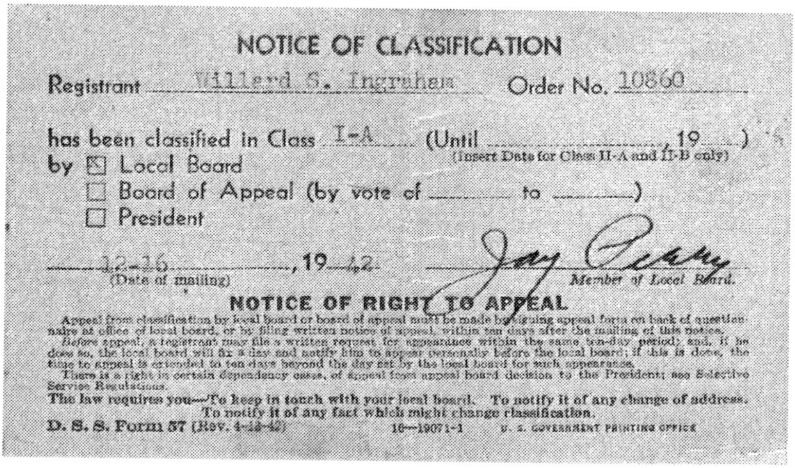

NOTICE OF CLASSIFICATION

Registrant Willard S. Ingraham Order No. 10860

has been classified in Class I-A (Until ...., 19...)
(Insert Date for Class II-A and II-B only)

by ☒ Local Board
☐ Board of Appeal (by vote of .... to ....)
☐ President

12-16, 1942
(Date of mailing)

Member of Local Board.

NOTICE OF RIGHT TO APPEAL

Appeal from classification by local board or board of appeal must be made by signing appeal form on back of questionnaire at office of local board, or by filing written notice of appeal, within ten days after the mailing of this notice.

Before appeal, a registrant may file a written request for appearance within the same ten-day period; and, if he does so, the local board will fix a day and notify him to appear personally before the local board; if this is done, the time to appeal is extended to ten days beyond the day set by the local board for such appearance.

There is a right in certain dependency cases, of appeal from appeal board decision to the President; see Selective Service Regulations.

The law requires you—To keep in touch with your local board. To notify it of any change of address. To notify it of any fact which might change classification.

D. S. S. Form 57 (Rev. 4-23-42) 16—19071-1 U. S. GOVERNMENT PRINTING OFFICE

I received a notice, in the mail, of my classification on December 16, 1942. I was classified as I-A, ready to go. I had to wait to find out what the next step would be that brought me closer to going into the service.

I do not remember the exact date, but sometime in January of 1943 I was to report to Spokane, Washington for my final physical examination and be inducted into the branch of service that the government deemed right. Others were reporting at the same time and all of us would be placed in the branch of the service we were needed at the time.

Upon arrival in Spokane at the induction place they ushered all of us into a large warehouse type building except it was very clean, well painted, very well lighted and adequately heated. There were numerous rooms leading from this large room all around the edge of this large room. Doctor stations circled the total room. I was getting my first glimpse of what army life was like.

There were, I guessed, well over two hundred of us that were all potential service applicants. We were all here for our final examination. They proceeded by ushering us into another room and telling us to strip naked and form a single line to start our procession through all of these doctor stations.

There was every type of doctor their to check every part of your body. To make it more interesting they would throw in an immunization shot line. Also we stopped along the way to give them a urine sample for a test.

Some big wise guys in line teased us about the big square needle we would get for one of our shots. We were all nervous about that shot. What surprised us was what happened when some of these wise guys that were smarting off stepped up to the station to get a shot in both arms at the same time. It was obvious to the rest of us that they were only trying to bolster their own courage to make it through the shot line. Sure enough, as they stepped up for their turn to get their shot some did not even look around but fell flat on the floor, out cold. Many of us coming up behind them when we saw what happened wondered if what they had said about that square needle might have some truth in it.

It took us most of the day to go through that line. When we finished we were told to put our clothes on and go through another line to determine what branch of service we would be assigned to. They had a rule in this line that every fifteenth person that was physically fit could choose between the army, navy or marines.

I was one of those lucky ones to have a choice. Quickly, my thinking was that my brother, Norman, was already in the army so maybe I would be sent to his camp in the army. With this in mind, my choice was army. Many times in the next three years I would wonder why I made that choice.

The next day we were sent to a different building where we were sworn in to the branch of service that we had selected. After being sworn in we were given a speech concerning our lives in the service. After that we were released to go to our respective homes to wait for orders to where we would be sent. We were now in the service with no uniform, waiting notice

WILLARD INGRAHAM, January 1943

My next notice came about the first of March informing me to be in front of Riches Café in Prosser at 3:00 p.m. on the 18th of March 1943. From this point I would catch a bus that took others and me to the train. My mind was racing thinking of where I would be sent, what part of the United States would I be sent to get my training and what kind of future would unfold in the coming years.

On the 18th of March I packed my clothes, a small shaving kit, soap and tooth brush all into a small suitcase. They had told us to pack light because all our civilian clothes would be sent back home once we were issued army clothes.

My Dad, Mother and sister Lorraine took me to Prosser to catch the bus. There were about a dozen of us eighteen year olds sent from this same small town on that day. Robert Ingraham, my cousin, also went out in this group

My Mother, bless her, tried so hard to hold a brave front without crying. She did while we were waiting for the bus but I looked back as I was boarding the bus and saw she could not hold it any longer. Looking out of the window of the bus I could see she was not the only Mother gathered there that was crying. It was hard for Mothers to think that this might be the last time they would ever see their sons.

Robert Ingraham

The bus took us to the train station where we all boarded the train. We did not go far when they sidetracked the train at Wallula Junction, which now is part of the Columbia River. Later in the sixties the McNary Dam was built and flooded all of the old Wallula Junction area where our train stopped that day. The new Wallula was moved back about three miles from where it once stood.

We were parked at the junction most of the night while they brought more passenger cars in and connected them to

McNary Dam

19

our passenger train. Sometime in the night they brought an engine and connected all the passenger cars and pulled us away. Late in the day of March 19th we ended up in Salt Lake City, Utah.

They brought in buses and transported us to Fort Douglas, Utah. It was there that they issued our uniforms. I was assigned to a new army unit called the 526th Armored Infantry Battalion. It was the first of its kind to be organized. It was a self-contained unit consisting of four companies, company A, B, and C and headquarter Co. Altogether we would be approximately 1200 to 1500 soldiers strong. Each company was provided with half-tracks to transport the infantry soldiers, trucks to provide the supplies, medics and cooks to go wherever we were located.

The half-tracks had 50 caliber guns mounted on them. Some of the squads were mortar and machine gun trained with about 10 infantry soldiers per half-track. Soldiers on each half-track, when trained, made a very strong fighting combat unit. Interesting to note is that our units in World War II were the same method for combat units now used in Iraq.

We were stationed at Fort Douglas for about three days. The barracks consisted of two story open buildings with about forty soldiers sleeping side by side on upper and lower cots on each floor making about 80 soldiers per building.

Everything was so new and so many orders flying around that a person wondered what was coming next. One thing they taught us was the chain of command and the rank of each person of non-commissioned and commissioned officers and the authority they held. The first day I was coming out of the barracks I met a corporal coming into the barracks. He looked at me then ordered me to go sweep the sidewalks; this I did immediately. The sidewalk was clean and needed no sweeping so I pretended for a while then took the broom back.

The soldier that slept on the bunk above me had been in the army before and held the rank of sergeant so he gave me tips concerning the army. The next day he gave me an example.

A corporal came upstairs and was showing off his authority, knowing we were all green civilians. The ex sergeant in my upper bunk told him to get lost. The corporal started over to our bunk when the ex sergeant told the corporal that he had been in this man's army before and knew all about it so now you, talking to the corporal, "get the hell down those stairs before I throw you down." The corporal stopped abruptly, looked at the ex sergeant and went quickly down the stairs. I learned an important lesson on this demonstration that is if you have rank and authority you had better darn well be prepared to back it up.

Our time at Fort Douglas, Utah was now finished. We were ready to go to our new destination. We were a different bunch of men now because we all had army haircuts, all dressed in army uniforms and had done every thing by command.

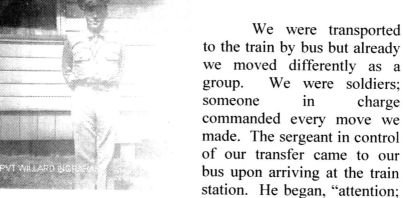

PVT WILLARD INGRAHAM

We were transported to the train by bus but already we moved differently as a group. We were soldiers; someone in charge commanded every move we made. The sergeant in control of our transfer came to our bus upon arriving at the train station. He began, "attention;

21

all of you will get off this bus and line up along side of the bus."

We marched all the way to the train's passenger car then halted and by command began to board the train. We had been told what seats we would be sitting in before we were dismissed. Later at mealtime a small group at a time would go down through the other passenger cars full of soldiers until we got to the dining car. We filled up our army food tray then headed on back to our passenger car and the seats we had been assigned to. The next group would go to the dining car and so on until all were fed.

The train was traveling along while all of this was going on. At night a porter came by and put our sleeper bed down so we, at least, had a bed to sleep in while on this journey. We remained in this same passenger car all the way to our destination. Our railroad car would be shifted to different sidetracks and another engine would attach to our passenger cars and away we would go until we reached our destination.

Our destination, of course, was Fort Knox, Kentucky. They took us right into Fort Knox before we debarked from the train. Buses were waiting for us when we arrived to take us to our barracks. It was the beginning of a very interesting and challenging next three years.

CHAPTER III:

BASIC TRAINING

On March 20, 1943 the newly selected cadres from the 480th Armored Infantry Regiment from Camp Campbell, Kentucky arrived at Fort Knox, Kentucky. Those cadres formed into the 1st armored group under Cornel Earl C Horan.

These cadres would be the sergeants to train these new units called the 526, 527 and the 528 Armored Infantry Battalions. All of these units were immediately activated.

All of these groups were the brainchild of Lieutenant General Lesley J. McNair, U.S. Army ground forces commander. The new units were made up of armored infantry, armored artillery and tank battalions designed to serve as temporary armored divisions when combined together with service and support units under a headquarters.

The official history states that this idea did not work in practice and due to manpower shortages in other units. All but one of the separate armored infantry battalions was disbanded in 1943. The 526 Armored Infantry went on to fight through WW II and proved to be a very effective combat unit.

 The first two weeks at Fort Knox we were all quarantined to our barracks and could not leave them except to go to the mess hall to eat or go out to the street for basic commands. Basic commands given were such as line up and go to the squads we were assigned to. The sergeant would say, "dress right dress,"

FORT KNOX BARRICKS That did not mean to go put on

clothes. It meant when you were lined up in three or four rows facing the sergeant in the street you would put your left arm straight out to your left side and look right then each one of us would keep that arm distance from each other. Then came the order left face; everyone turned to the left; forward march left two three four, hup, hup, hup, two three four; left two three four. When the sergeant got most of us in step and marching he sang out, "you are in the army now and not behind the plow, hup, two, three, four and so forth.

This book will refer to events that happened mostly in A Company of the 526 Armored Infantry Battalion with the second platoon of A Company of the 526 Armored Infantry Battalion. We had many briefings on what was expected and the type of weapons we would be trained to use. We did not have the use of half-tracks while we trained at Fort Knox.

L to R: S/Sgt Gribble, S/Sgt Crompton and S/Sgt Lowe

Ranks of the following were Platoon leader 2nd platoon, I/Lt Harry Willyard, platoon sergeant T/Sgt Leonard Landholt,

Hq. Squad, S/Sgt John Gribble, 1st Squad S/Sgt Raymond Dykes, 2nd squad S/Sgt Marcus Wright, Machine Gun Squad S/Sgt Dewey Lowe, and Mortar Squad S/Sgt Charles Crumpton. 2nd Lt Charles Wilkinson was our platoon leader at first at Fort Knox. Raymond Dykes and Marcus Wright made S/Sgt later on, maybe in Europe. Raymond Dykes went on to fight in the Korean War and there he was killed.

The 526 Armored Infantry Battalion consisted of: Battalion Commander Lt. Col. Carlisle B. Irwin, Headquarters Company Capt. Robert Curts, Service Company Capt. Klinker, Medial Detachment Capt. Berlin, A Company Capt. Charles Mitchel, B Company Capt. Wessels, C Company Capt. Gianelloni. Each company at full strength consisted of about 250 soldiers. Battalion strength consisted of 1200 to 1500 soldiers.

Lt. Victor Maeef was A Company Commander for the first month or two then Lt. Charles Mitchell became A Company Comander and soon he was promoted to Capt. Robert Elkins was A Company's first sergeant at first then he got promoted to Warrant Officer and transferred out. Wm. Lowry became A Company's First Sergeant.

It was hot at this time of year at Fort Knox so everyone was issued the army summer khaki uniforms. They taught us the correct way to salute the officers. It may seem unimportant to emphasize the salute except to say if you did not hold your thumb down close to your hand when you made a snappy salute your thumb would most likely hit your eye. A sharp jab in the eyeball could

Summer dress 1943 prove to be injurious to the eye.

We also learned to accomplish all commands when holding our rifles as in parade rest, port arms, salute, aim, fire and sling arms and so on. We would march out to the shooting range and fire all day at targets at 100 yards, 300 yards and 500 yards distance in a prone position, sitting position and standing position. At the end of the day we would march back

Learning to salute correctly to our barracks, many miles distance. After getting toughened in we began the 30-mile a day march and it became a routine thing to do.

After the quarantine was over we could go to the PX to buy candy etc. The PX was a post exchange where one could buy many things without the tax price on the articles. We also got weekend passes to Louisville, Kentucky and other cities within about 100 miles of Fort Knox.

There was a good bus connection out of Fort Knox so it was easy to get to where one wanted to go. In Louisville there were many choices of

Port Arms

things to do like going to the YMCA building where they had bowling, dancing or just go to the large recreation room. There were many stuffed chairs and tables if you wanted to use your time to write letters back home. Writing was my choice as it was very relaxing and it gave me the time to relax and get my mind together.

Ingraham and Williams

Boyce Williams and I went on many weekend passes together. One week though I decided to stay in my barracks to get caught up on letter writing and just relax. There were only a few of us that decided to stay. We soon found out why it was not a good idea to hang around the barracks on the weekend. In came the corporal on duty for the weekend looking for someone to do kitchen duty or some other detail. I think they discouraged anyone to stay in the barracks on the weekend because they always found plenty of duties for those that stayed. You can bet I never stayed around the barracks any more on my time off.

One day we had just completed a 30-mile hike out to an area to run maneuvers with competing forces to take a chosen objective and our group was going through rough terrain. We were carrying our guns and full field pack on our backs when we came to a dry creek bed and had to jump down into the bottom of the creek bed. I jumped down and landed on a rough rock; my ankle popped like a gunshot. Needless to say I couldn't get up. Our lieutenant said he heard the pop and knew I was in trouble. He checked my ankle and discovered my ankle was swelling up fast. He used his knife and cut the tongue of my shoe so he could pull my shoe off. There was a medic jeep there that took me back to Fort Knox to the medic building. A doctor checked me and told me to go back to the barracks and soak my ankle in as hot water as I could stand then throw out the hot water and use cold water to soak the ankle. I was to repeat this every hour until I went to bed.

Back in the barracks I found I was the only one there as the rest of the company was out in the bivouac area. That night it thundered, lightening and rained very hard all night. A thought ran through my mind that maybe I lucked out by not being out there in the mud and rain.

The next morning I went on sick call to the medics because my ankle and leg was all swollen up like a balloon. The corporal at the medics told me to go to the hospital. I asked him if he could take me there as I knew the hospital was over a mile away. He said there were no jeep available and I would have to walk there.

It was a long mile that I had to walk. I had to walk with many stops along the way. By this time my ankle and leg felt like a piece of lead and every time I stepped on that leg a sharp pain would shoot up my leg that was already swollen. When I got to the hospital there was about 30 soldiers already lined up to go in for various reasons. A nurse came out of the hospital with a clipboard and was taking notes and names from each of us down the line. When she got to me she asked what my problem was. I told her I had sprained my ankle. She said, "Let me see." She took one look at my leg and said, "you come with me." She took me ahead of all the others that were in the sick line. Immediately I was taken to a doctor's office and the doctor checked me over. He said something to the nurse that I couldn't hear. The nurse disappeared and soon came back with a wheel chair. I looked at the wheel chair and told them that I had walked over a mile to the hospital so if I had to stay here I sure did not need a wheel chair to go to my room. He told me that I may have walked a mile up here but I was to sit in that chair so I could be taken to a room where I would be staying for a while. They took me to a dormitory room and put me to bed with two pillows under my leg and told me not to move. If I needed anything they would get it including a bedpan.

I lay on my back with the pillows under my leg for three days. I would wait until the nurse went to her little office at the end of the dormitory room and then I would go down to the bathroom. I never did ask the nurse for a bedpan. The nurse caught me one day on my way back to my bed. She read the right act to me. My stay at the hospital was about three weeks.

When I got back to my unit I had to toughen up in a hurry because they were still doing the 30-mile hikes plus now we went on forced marches in that hot humid weather in Kentucky. On these 30-mile excursions we normally

Farm Boy To Soldier

bivouacked over night. During this time we discovered that the area was full of little bugs called chiggers. They are little bugs like a mite that one can't see but when they get on you they chew, making you itch all over.

One day out in the bivouacked area I caught a little mouse that had long legs and looked like a deer. In fact, that is what they were called, a deer mouse. They were only about two inches tall.

By now we had checked out with shooting our guns on the shooting range. We had shot the 30-caliber machine gun, the 50-caliber machine gun, the 30-caliber carbine and the 45-caliber pistol. We were judged on how well we could shoot all of these guns and given a medal as an expert, sharp shooter or marksman. One day the sergeant called us together and said he needed ten volunteer drivers. Many of us stepped up for that chance. The sergeant said, "you, you, you," and so on counting off ten of us. He continued, "All ten of you go to the supply sergeant and check out ten brooms and drive them down this street until it is clean." He was hard pressed to get any volunteers after that.

One time at Fort Knox I received a new 1943 copper penny change from a purchase. I thought that was strange because all the pennies I had seen that were made in 1943 were lead pennies. I kept this 1943 as my good luck piece and carried it as a good luck charm all the years I was in the army. I still have the penny. When I was discharged I found out these copper pennies were worth a lot of money. I dug my penny out of my keepsakes and discovered that on the date only the 194 was visible. From carrying this penny all that time the 3 was worn off so it could not be seen. I still keep it as a lucky piece.

Fort Knox has an interesting history. In 1932 congress designed Fort Knox to be a permanent garrison. Later the treasure department selected a portion of Fort Knox as the sight for the gold depository for the treasure department of the United States government. Construction followed and the vault was built. In 1936 the US bullion depository was completed and the first gold shipments arrived at Fort Knox between January and June 1937. When we were on our 30-mile walk we would pass by the big gold vault.

U. S. Gold Depository, Fort Knox, Kentucky

One day a rumor was passed down that they were looking for soldiers to transfer to the paratroopers. It seemed to grab a lot of us so as a large group we went to the company commander's office to volunteer to go to the paratroopers. The brass was not anticipating anything like this to happen so they told us to forget it. We would not be going to the paratroopers. We never heard any more about the paratroopers after that.

Mail call was so important to all of us to receive letters from back home. I felt sorry for some of the soldiers. They would come every day to see if a letter had come and have but another disappointed. I always received a lot of letters so

seeing the sad looks on the ones that hardly ever got a letter
made me feel sad for them.

Chow Line at Fort Knox, Kentucky

Eating time for all of us was an elating time of
anticipation, as we would wait in long lines starting at the door
of the mess hall and down the street. When the door opened it
did not take long to line up in front of the chow line to fill our
trays then go to the tables and eat the food while it was hot.
Some would always complain about the food but I never
thought the food was that bad.

**Lt/Col
Carlisle B. Irwin**

Lt. Col. Carlisle Irwin
526 Armored Infantry Battalion
Commander and a few times
in the nine months we served
at Fort Knox ordered all the
battalions out on the parade
ground for a battalion
inspection. He would whiz
up and down the rows of
soldiers in each company like
he was going to a race. When
he inspected each individual
company he would do the
same. By the speed he

inspected the rows of soldiers we nick named him Lt. Col. Irwin, P40. As you know the P40 fighter plane in the 40's was a very fast plane. If someone spotted Lt. Col. Irwin coming they would say, "here comes P40," and everyone knew who they meant. The name stuck all through the war years.

The street inspection wasn't bad but when he came to our barracks and put on his white gloves we knew we were in trouble and usually were. After he inspected our barracks with white gloves it was on our knees scrubbing the floors that night.

My squad leader was S/Sgt John Gribble who was twenty-six years old. We all called him an old man because most of us were eighteen-year-old farm boys.

Some of us at this time didn't have enough whiskers to shave but the lieutenant insisted everyone would shave everyday. Most of us came from Washington, Idaho and California.

The marches over agony hill in the humid hot Kentucky sun with only one

S/Sgt. John Gribble

canteen of water to drink put a strain on our bodies. I would remember the long work days in the fields in the humid hot sun of North Dakota where I grew up as a boy and thought this is not any worse than those times. The army required that we take a salt tablet each day.

Our favorite time was to march out to the firing range and shoot our weapons. By now we were all qualified to shoot any of the thirty and fifty caliber guns that was used for training at Fort Knox. We continued doing the thirty-mile marches. There would be a five-minute break once in a while along the way. When we stopped for these breaks we would hit the ground and immediately go to sleep. There would always be some pranksters who would catch you asleep and stick a match in the sole of your shoe and light it. It wasn't long the recipient of that match jumped up cussing and swearing to catch the person that did that. Everyone accepted it good naturedly because we knew that the time would come when we found out who set that match and his turn would come.

WAACS at Right Dress

By now we had discovered that there was a company of WAACS stationed at Fort Knox. The WAACS were women soldiers. They were hard working and helped in many ways to do their part in the war. You might have guessed it, that section of Fort Knox was closed to any male soldier.

It was always a pleasure to go to the bus station in Louisville, Kentucky. It was a very modern and efficient operated bus terminal.

We could always depend on good connections to go wherever we wanted to go. One night the 526, 527 and 528 Armored Infantry Battalions were on our many night training missions when some of the scouting patrols got over into the area X that was top secret and no trespassing. The scouting patrol was unaware that they had entered a restricted area. They viewed an unbelievable sight occurring there. Apparently the patrol was from 528 Armored Infantry Battalion but the security did not know how many of all our units had witnessed the new phenomenon in the secret training area. Immediately in the following days the 527 and the 528 Armored Infantry Battalions were inactivated with some of their units being transferred into the 526 Armored Infantry Battalion and others transferred out elsewhere.

Farm Boy To Soldier

The 526 Armored Infantry Battalion was the first armored infantry battalion to be activated. It was now the sole separate armored infantry battalion in the American army. Rumors were flying rampant so when we would hear a new rumor we would ask which stool did you get this one from. Finally we got some positive information telling us that because of the encounter with the secret unit in area X we would now be soon going to the Arizona desert and be attached to the new mysterious unit.

Completes Basic Training

Pvt. Willard S. Ingraham, son of Mr. and Mrs. Lyle Ingraham has finished 13 weeks of basic training at Fort Knox, Kentucky, and is now classed as a "line soldier" of the Armored Force.

Besides being instructed in the basic principles of the army the men in the armored group have been given special training in the care and use of arms and equipment. They have been taught how to fire pistols, rifles and machine guns and have drilled and hiked so much that a 25 mile march seems almost easy, according to those familiar with the training.

The 526 Armored Infantry had now completed our basic training and were ready for our training in maneuvers in practice of assimilated war problems. Soon orders were issued to pack our equipment and our bag and make ready for our move.

The 526 Armored Infantry Battalion left Fort Knox on September 14, 1943. We arrived in Bouse, Arizona five days later on September 19, 1943.

36

CHAPTER IV:

HAPPY VALLEY

The 526 Armored Infantry Battalion left the train at Bouse, Arizona. Bouse looked like a stopping place in the desert in the middle of nowhere. It was a whistle stop station with a sidetrack to switch railroad cars.

Trucks that had been waiting took us down a twenty-mile dusty road to our place for training called, "Camp Bouse." It was an empty place with indications of surveying that had previously been made to identify streets and so on.

The trucks that brought us in were also packed with tents that had been loaded at Bouse. The first order was to get all the tents up. Eight

1984 This is how Camp Bouse is now and how it looked before Camp Bouse tents

soldiers for each tent installation was lined up on the tentive street and each group would take a tent to each selected tent space. It was amazing how a bare spot in the desert soon became a tent city.

The next day a truck detail was sent to Needles, California to pick up a load of lumber. The lumber consisted mostly of 2 x 4 by 8 foot to be used for framing that would be the kitchen. There was 2 x 6 x 16 foot lumber to build the roof for the kitchen and a big tent to cover the structure for the roof.

Also we dug trenches down along the street about six inches deep and installed a one inch galvanized line of pipe to the water source. It very quickly supplied running water to the kitchen.

Pfc. Willard Ingraham   Pfc. Lincoln Mahaffey

The next day we were informed that anyone who had fifteen dollars and was eligible could go on furlough. This would be our first furlough we had since entering the army. The problem was that many did not have money and were disappointed. I had saved a small amount of money and gave several soldiers each fifteen dollars so they could go on furlough. Now I was down to my last fifteen dollars. That meant I would have to hitch hike a ride to Salt Lake City, Utah then the fifteen dollars would get me a train ticket to Kennewick, Washington and home.

Lincoln Mahaffey of B company, 526 Armored Infantry Battalion was going to Kennewick, Washington where his parents lived so we paired up to go that far together. The army trucks took us to Parker, Arizona and from there everyone was on their own. Lincoln and I immediately walked to the edge of town. It was a very small town and we had to wait for cars going by that would pick us up. There was not much crime at this time so people were always helpful in picking up soldiers and giving them a lift if they could.

We had not waited long until two ladies stopped to pick us up. Guess where they were going? You guessed it, to Salt Lake City, Utah. We hadn't traveled very long when the lady that was driving asked Lincoln if he minded driving. He said, "not at all," and drove all the way to Salt Lake City. It was late that night when we got to Salt Lake City and Lincoln drove right to the railroad station.

We had enough money to get train fare to Kennewick. At that late time of night the station was open but no one there to give us the tickets. We soon found out that the train would not be coming until morning. Lincoln and I tried to get some sleep on the benches in the station but a night guard told us that no one could sleep there and kept waking us up periodically. About the third time we were getting rather irritable about his abruptness and told him so.

When morning came we were on the train and on our way to Kennewick. Upon our arrival in Kennewick we agreed to meet again in two weeks for our return trip to Camp Bouse. My parents lived at Prosser, Washington so I had another thirty-five miles to hitch hike. I had no problem catching a ride. When I arrived at Prosser my parents' place was four miles out of Prosser but someone gave me a ride home.

I spent a very happy two weeks at home with my parents. I had not sold my car when I entered service so I had wheels while I was at home. In 1943 there was gas rationing so people were allotted different amounts of gas ration coupons. I went down to city hall in Prosser to get coupons for gas and they would only give enough coupons to get five gallons of gas. They told me they could only give me enough gas coupons to get me back and forth to where I was staying. I told them "thanks a whole lot."

Pvt Arnold Steffens

Soon the furlough was over and my parents took me to Kennewick where I met Lincoln. We caught the train that night and were in Salt Lake City, Utah the next day.

I had prearranged to meet my cousin, Arnold Steffens, at Kerns Air Force Base where he was stationed. Kerns Air Force Base is just outside of Salt

Lake City. While we were together we discussed the possibility of selling our farm because neither of us knew what might happen to us before the war would be over. We decided that it would be best under our circumstances to go ahead and put the farm up for sale. Later when I got back to camp I wrote to my parents and asked them if they would sell our farm. They did sell it for twice as much as we had paid for it. We felt pretty good about doubling our money on that investment.

My short visit with Arnold was soon over so back to the Salt Lake City railroad station Lincoln and I went and on our way again. The closest we could get to Bouse with those connections was Salome, Arizona. From that point there were no more railroad connections. We had to hitch hike to Bouse. It was not easy to do but we finally made it back to Camp Bouse.

There had been a lot of changes in camp since we had left on our furloughs. The 526 Armored Infantry Battalion was now attached to the Ninth Tank Group commanded by Colonel Joseph Gilbreth. It was composed of the 701, 736, 737, 739, 740 and 748 tank battalions. This was the same mysterious group that had been isolated in a remote part of Fort Knox known as Area X. It was the same group that the 526, 527 and 528 Armored Infantry Battalions encountered on that night training mission at Fort Knox, Kentucky.

American officers including General Dwight D. Eisenhower had seen a demonstration of the CDLS in October, 1942 and as a result exercises started at the armored training center at Fort Knox, Kentucky. The training site had been designated Area X. From Area X the battalions and its parent unit, the ninth tank group headed to Camp Bouse, Arizona for training. The battalions arrived at the camp in Arizona's Butler Valley in mid September 1943. For the 526 Armored Infantry it would be the beginning of six months intensive training that was to become known as **Happy Valley**.

Camp Bouse was the mystery post of CAMA (California Arizona Maneuver area). People outside of Bouse would comment there is something very mysterious going on in there because we see a lot of soldiers going in but never coming out. They did not know how right they were because out of the six months we were in Camp Bouse for training we had only three week-end passes out of there.

Beginning in October mail was censored and given an APO address. Soldiers were not allowed to leave camp except in small groups led by a non commissioned officer or an officer. Soldiers were sworn to secrecy and threatened with death if they disclosed anything about the Gizmos or our training with them. We called these tanks Gizmos or man made moon light tanks.

On our first weekend pass to Phoenix, Arizona there was one pass for one lieutenant, three sergeants and eleven soldiers. Can you imagine fifteen soldiers with one pass that all must stay together to make sure that no one would talk? Did you ever try to get a room for fifteen? When we had to go to the bathroom there had to be at least two of us there. Needless to say, it was almost a disaster, especially when all of us started to drink. Oh yes, that was another problem. Did you ever go to a bar and get a table and chairs for fifteen. Also where in the 1940s could one go to a restaurant and get seating for fifteen. I am sure you get the picture.

The ride to Phoenix in itself was a nightmare. We all rode in the back of a truck over twenty miles of dusty, sand roads then another two hours to Phoenix in a truck packed with soldiers. Can you imagine what we looked like when we got there? We were all burned brown by the Arizona sun and all well muscled and looked rugged. We probably were at that time and felt just as tough.

The second weekend pass to Phoenix was different but still not workable. We were given one pass for a sergeant and four soldiers. Again, have you ever been able to get a room for five and so on? Needless to say it did not work out well either.

The last pass to Phoenix was a buddy pass that worked out the best of all. We still had our security in each other in case we began to drink and forget ourselves. This never happened though because by that time we were responsible enough to know the danger in the slip of the tongue.

Our desert camp, by now began to look pretty good. We had an outdoor movie that showed good movies, a post exchange to get our necessities. We also had beer that was warm but still tasted good. We had a tent chapel that we could attend unless we had other duties to perform. The walk from the door of the chapel to the street had rocks that were painted white that outlined the walkway.

Pfc. Bill Rogers

There was a boxing ring that was always popular. We would often go to root for Bill Rogers who was a participant in quite a few boxing matches. He came out with a lot of wins.

The tents that we quartered in were the pyramidal type. They held eight cots; two cots to a side with a pot bellied stove in the center with a stovepipe going up the center. It was common in the evenings to visit our buddy's in other tents. It got interesting when someone would toss a thirty-caliber shell in the stove and everyone would scatter. At least, the shell cleaned the soot out of the chimney.

Residences at Camp Bouse – "Happy Valley"

For a while there was another trick that some pulled. They would take the powder out of a grenade then when a group was formed for some reason they would throw the grenade amongst them. The grenade would sputter and smoke and spit; everyone was gone by that time because when someone yelled grenade everyone scattered lightening fast. This came to a stop when some new grenades came in that all of the powder could not be removed and it was possible for the grenade to explode.

When we arrived at Camp Bouse the 526 Armored Infantry Battalion had been issued new MI Garand Rifles. The rifle was gas operated, semi automatic and held eight shells. You could fire all the shells from the clip as fast as you could pull the trigger. When all the shells were gone from the clip, the clip automatically popped out of the rifle leaving you immediately ready to inject another clip of new shells into the gun. The rifle weighed about eleven pounds and with open sights you could fire up to five hundred yards fairly accurately.

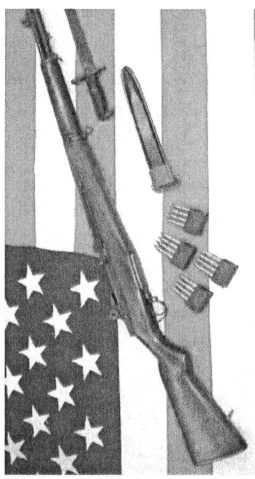

It was a very dependable gun. This gun was issued to all combat infantry soldiers that fought in WWII. These new guns came to us at Camp Bouse packed in cosmoleen, which is a grease to keep the rifles from rusting. This cosmoleen was very hard to remove. The rifle had to be completely disassembled, piece-by-piece, soaked and cleaned in gasoline. This job took all of us the better part of a day to complete.

Also at this same time, the 526 Armored Infantry Battalion was issued half-tracks, personnel carriers with tracks

M1 Garands Rifle

used for the rear wheels of the half-tracts. It was from this that the half-tracts got their name.

In mid 1943, the United States Army ordered the formation of a special tank group to be entirely manned by carefully screened, highly qualified volunteers that were stationed at Fort Knox, Kentucky. The order further stated that once selected to become a member of this elite unit future transfers were prohibited. They would train with a weapon that would change the course of the war. This special force was named the Ninth Tank Group. It consisted of six tank battalions, 701, 737, 738, 739, 740 and 748 tank battalions and one infantry battalion, the 526 Armored Infantry Battalion.

A team of officers was sent to the desert training center in southeastern California to locate a training site for this unique group. The team determined that Butler Valley in the Arizona desert, 20 miles Northeast of the small town of Bouse, Arizona would be the ideal location for the Ninth Tank group to train in absolute secrecy for participation in the British developed "Canal Defense Light." CDL or gizmo as the soldiers called it.

1943 – 1944 work began in late August to ready the camp for operations. By mid September, it became a large tent city complex. Camp Bouse that we called **Happy Valley** was the mystery post of the California, Arizona maneuver area. The CDLs' were to illuminate a battlefield and blind and disorient an enemy with a carbine arc lamp that produced 13-million candlepower. A normal carbon arc lamp with a reflector that was parabolic in its vertical axis and elliptical on the horizontal axis producing a beam that converged and subsequently diverged from a nodal point some 60 to 70 inches away from the source of light. This beam was reflected half way down its primary focus by an ordinary flat reflecting of polished aluminum. The effect of the two reflectors was that the arc lamp could be mounted behind armor and the beam emitted at the point where the beam converged. In this case it was through a slot two inches in width and 24 inches in height. An automatic shutter would create a flickering effect that would further confuse an enemy so that they could not get an accurate range on the CDL.

The command, "scatter," would be given to commence the flicker effect which would keep the iris constantly trying to adjust to rapid changes, six cycles per second, between light and dark. The light operator could change the colors of the light to amber, (sun), or blue, (moon) with different color screens. The amber screen made the light look close and the blue screen made the light appear in the distance. The lights in the tanks would flash amber and blue. If both lights, at once, an enemy would become disoriented and could not tell the exact location of the lights or the tanks.

The tactic was straight forward. Fifteen CDLs would advance abreast of each other with thirty yards between each tank. In a cone of darkness, behind the CDLs, regular tanks called fighter tanks accompanied by infantry would advance on an enemy position. The light itself was a carbon arc light consisting of thirteen thousand candle power. A drive shaft from the transmission drove a generator that supplied the electricity needed to activate the carbon arc. A concave mirror was mounted behind the arc light at the rear of the turret. This mirror could be adjusted to precisely focus and intensify the light through the slot and onto the terrain in front of the tank from as far away as fifteen hundred yards.

Most of our training was at night with those man made moonlight tanks or gizmos as most of us called them. In some exercises the infantry would be lined out in front of these tanks in night training. The tanks would be coming toward us with those flickering lights. There was no way you could guess at what distance they were from you. It is true, you could hear the clanking of the tanks but not how close they were and where they were in that darkness.

We were told that with live ammunition we could shoot at the tanks when we felt we could get a hit on the tanks. After

47

the exercises they would count the bullet hits on the tanks to see how effective the CDLs were.

Desert floor/Camp Bouse

We also ran exercises with the CDLs and our infantry group going forward with the CDLs under the cloak of darkness to see how effective the CDLs would be with the enemy out front. From the protection of the cloaks of darkness it was possible to see out front hundred of yards forward.

Rattle-snake

We ran many night maneuvers with the half-tracks against Chocolate Drop Hill. We fired so many bullets into that hill I think they should have called it lead hill. We would go so far in the half-track then dismount and charge the hill flopping on our stomachs over and over again. The desert floor was always covered with cactus needles and stickers; you didn't know if when you flopped down you might be landing on a rattle snake, a scorpion or be lucky to land on just the sticky cactus needles.

We also got a lot of practice out in the shooting range. We mostly shot our MI rifles but also the thirty-caliber machine gun and the new one called the bar, Browning automatic rifle. This Browning must have been about fifteen pounds in weight with a thirty-shell clip so if you aimed at something and held the trigger down it would empty the full clip of shells in seconds.

We would also get behind some barrier then they would fire bullets over our heads. We would try to identify what

49

caliber bullet passed over our head by the sound of it passing. After a while we all could identify the bullet that was shot.

One night we were taken out to a place in the open desert where they had pre-dug a trench about four foot deep and maybe three hundred feet long. We were told to get down in this trench and stay there until we were told to crawl out of the trench carefully because there would be machine guns that would be firing bullets and tracers over the whole crawling area. The bullets, they told us, would be about eighteen inches over us so whatever we did don't stand up until we got to the end of the obstacle course which I imagine was about one hundred yards. Now, mind you, this was at night with tracer bullets flying that close over your head. We were sure those bullets were coming right at us.

Cactus thorns

The desert floor that we were crawling over was full of cactus thorns and stickers. Not only that but as we were crawling down across this section there was explosive charges being set off around us every so often. As I was crawling along there was a small sunken place in the ground; I was going to crawl right through it rather than crawl around it. John Kalisek was ahead of me and looking back he saw what I was about to do; he yelled at me to get out of there because that was where one of those explosives charges was placed. I no more got passed that hole when a big charge went off by my feet throwing sand and needles all over me.

The explosive charges and cactus needles was not the only thing that we had to be concerned about but also rattlesnakes and scorpions.

After crawling through this obstacle course it took us a week to pick out the cactus needles that embedded into our arms, legs and stomach. I heard after this exercise that one soldier did freak out and stood up going through the course. I do not know this as truth but only as a rumor and rumors in that place were always flying.

One day several of us were standing around when we noticed a cactus growing on a knoll in the desert about eight hundred yards away. We challenged S/Sgt John Gribble to try to shoot and hit that cactus at that distance. He took careful

51

aim and fired. We all saw a puff of dust rise off the top of that cactus.

The cactus plants were very good target practice for throwing knives. I purchased a very nice throwing knife from our camp PX. It had a nice leather belt sheath to carry the knife. I traced the jungle girl, Sheena, on the leather and found something to put some color on the tracing of Sheena. It turned out good. I kept the knife until the end of the war then gave it to Bill Rogers. As far as I know he still has the knife.

The day came and it was time for our booster shots. After that took place there was always some joker that would hit your arm on top of the shot. He knew very well that when he made that hit there would always be one coming back to him.

Lt. Willyard trained us how to defend ourselves with Judo classes. We practiced how to grab our opponent and throw him over our shoulder so fast he would not have a chance to counter act your move. We learned judo chops and other moves. By practicing everyday we got pretty good at it.

Lt. Willyard told us now that we had self-defense pretty good we will see what you can do with someone with a rifle. He showed us the self-protecting moves and how to put the person with the rifle at a disadvantage. The unexpected quick moves on our part were the secret.

Next, the lieutenant told us to install our bayonet on the barrel of our rifle leaving the scabbard on the bayonet. He demonstrated to us how, if someone came at us with a bayonet, we could soon take that gun and bayonet away from him. We got fairly good doing that so he told us to now remove the scabbard from the bayonet. He said, "ah – ha, that makes a difference now doesn't it with that twelve inch sharp bayonet pointed right at you looking mighty wicked."

He went on to tell us that it was because we did not know how to counter a sharp pointed knife that was pointed in our direction. He told us he would show us how to defend ourselves so that we would not be afraid of a knife bayonet. He did teach us what to do but that sharp point on that bayonet always looked mighty intimidating.

We practiced those defenses many days to where we would not be as afraid of a sharp knife coming at us. The problem was if your apponent also had a plan of defense someone was going to get hurt.

Next, the lieutenant said, "what if you found yourself without ammunition or a bayonet with you at the time but had a piece of piano wire? You would have a lethal weapon."

His favorite saying was, "you then take this wire and put it around your opponent's neck and give it a pull. The head will roll down the street singing, "I ain't got no body."

Pfc John Kalisek and
Pfc Willard Ingraham

Most of our training at Camp Bouse was at night so we would sleep during the day when it was hot. We rolled the sides of the tents up and a breeze would blow through our tent. We were out of the sun and had a breeze blowing so it never got unbearable from the heat.

We did not train with the CDLs every night so on our off time we watched the movies

, went for a few beers etc. One night we heard a shot ring out in our camp. We all wondered what happened because that was unusual for someone to shoot inside the camp. The next morning we got the story about what had happened. It seems this sergeant from C company, 526 Armored Infantry Battalion did not want to go to the show that night intending to get some extra sleep. As he was lying there in his cot, in the dark, he thought he heard the flap of the tent open. He did not see anyone enter his tent so dismissed the thought. Shortly he realized something touched the side of his cot. He looked over and there was an animal with its paws on his cot staring down on him. He had a forty- five pistol under his pillow so he slowly collected the gun in his hand and shot the animal. It turned out to be a bob- cat that had come into camp. I did not believe the story when I heard so I walked over to C company to check the story out. Sure enough, there lay the dead bobcat that had obviously been shot.

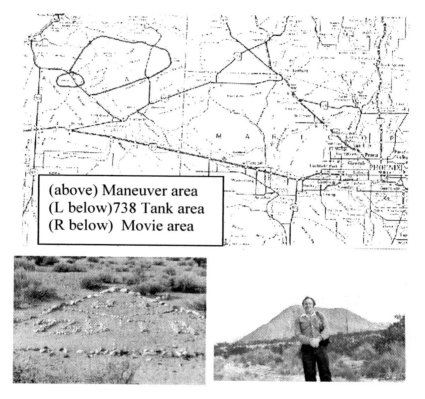

(above) Maneuver area
(L below)738 Tank area
(R below) Movie area

There were a lot of rumors flying around that we would soon be moving out of this camp. Our training was apparently winding down as it was noted that there was more time to go for walks. We walked out where there were bigger cactus plants and practiced throwing our knives at them. The cactus plants made excellent targets to practice knife throwing because it never damaged the knife and it was easy to pull out after the throw.

Our church tent at Camp Bouse was located here

As we anticipated, the word finally came down that we would soon be moving. We would be going to Fort Hamilton and from there over seas.

CHAPTER V:
A BATTLE ON THE HIGH SEAS

After receiving the port of embarkation notice it was a very busy time around Camp Bouse getting everything packed and ready to go. We knew we were headed for Fort Hamilton that was located on Staten Island in New York City.

All of the half-tracks, trucks, artillery guns and so forth had to be transported to Bouse. Everything was then loaded and tied down securely to flat bed railroad cars that were parked on a side-track. All of this took the better part of a week to accomplish.

After all the tents were struck and loaded we took a last look at the big desert that had been our home for the last six months. We all took with us many memories that would stay with us for our lifetime. We loaded up in trucks to ride down that long twenty-mile dusty road to Bouse. This was about the tenth of March 1944 and the very hot weather of Arizona had not yet arrived.

At Bouse we boarded a troop train carrying our duffle bag and our M1 Garand rifle. After living with the rifle for the past six months it seemed to be a part of our lives. The train moved us across country through several states. It took us five days to get to our destination. New Mexico and Texas was dry like Arizona. As we moved up through Arkansas and Missouri there were green fields starting to appear. In Illinois, Indiana, Ohio and Pennsylvania we saw more trees and rolling hills. After we got to New Jersey it wasn't long before we entered the Brooklyn Army base.

We made transfers here and proceeded to Fort Hamilton that was located on Staten Island. It was good to get off that train and get some exercise again. We were back in barracks and it was different than what we were used to. We were all very brown from the hot Arizona sun and quite a bit more rugged but we hadn't forgotten we were still house trained.

We found Fort Hamilton was and remains a very historical site. In 1664 England seized New Amsterdam from Holland and changed the colony's name to New York. English colonies ruled for more than a century. On July 4, 1776 a small American battery on the site of present day Fort Hamilton fired into the British Man O War ships conveying troops to suppress the American Revolution.

On June 11, 1825 the cornerstone granite went into place for Fort Lewis. It became Fort Hamilton later although references to the structures as Fort Hamilton occurred as early as 1826. It was not officially named until the 20th century.

In 1831, Battery F, 4th artillery, left Governors Island with two officers and fifty-two enlisted men that became Fort Hamilton's first garrison. The 27th regiment, New York Militia found a home at Fort Hamilton and began training. Captain Robert E. Lee was assigned to Fort Hamilton as the post engineer in 1841. In the 1850s Stonewall Jackson was assigned to Fort Hamilton.

During the Civil War, Fort Hamilton was a training site for volunteer regiments and the post strength reached as high as 1000 enlisted men. At the time of World War I the post became a processing point for hundred of thousands of American soldiers going to France.

In 1942 over three million soldiers were processed through the New York Port of embarkation for transport to Europe in World War II. At the close of hostilities Fort Hamilton also served as point of discharge for millions of returning troops. Fort Hamilton was placed under 1st army control in 1949. In 1974 the old fortress was designated a national historic landmark. In 1976 New York City recruiting battalion established at For Hamilton. The Military District Of Washington took over command of Fort Hamilton in 1998. Fort Hamilton is the U.S. Army's ambassador to New York City that serves 5000 full time active duty personnel.

We knew we would be at Fort Hamilton for eighteen days and we were going to make the most of everything. The days were busy with army business but our nights were ours. We took the New York subway and went all over New York City and New Jersey. At first we had passes but not every night so we discovered a hole in the wire fence and away we went.

Some of us were put on KP duty at the officers' area. We did not mind that at all because we could see how much better they ate than what we were given. While on KP we would do our work of peeling potatoes, etc but being out and about most of the nights we needed some sleep. When the work slowed down the sergeant cook would find us fast asleep on the flour sacks in the storage room.

Our passes had stopped so a sergeant marched about half a dozen of us up to the guard that was checking the gate and told him that we did not have passes but we were all going out. The guard hesitated for a while then stepped aside.

The CDLs were at the base and were being loaded onto the ships. Our A Company 526 Armored Infantry was selected to stand guard while the CDLs were loaded and secured by long shore men. We had to watch that none of the CDL tank covers were ever lifted to give anyone a chance to peek under the tarp. We also were night guards at the railroad tracks to see that no one came around the CDL tanks in any way. We had orders backed up clear to the president that if anyone messed around our secret and would not listen to our commands we were to shoot them with no hesitation.

When we would have a free night again we would march up to the guard post at the gate and go right on through. The guards got so they would just shake their heads as we marched by. They paid no attention to us on our return.

We also found the USO (United Service Organization) in New York where we spent quite a few nights dancing and enjoying life in New York City. I must say this was quite a change from the shut in desert life of Arizona.

Our secret was still to be honored and it was a death sentence if we should tell anyone of our training. By this time we were trusted; they knew we would not divulge our secret. One night I had the duty of guarding the CDL tanks as they were lifted onto the ship. When I went aboard the ship and was ready to relieve the guard that was on duty I immediately threw a live round into the chamber of my gun. It wasn't long and here came the captain of the ship with two SP (shore patrol police). The captain's face was red and very angry. He said, "there is no one that will have a loaded gun on my ship." He further told me that the SP did not walk around with a loaded gun and he wanted me to immediately unload my gun.

I said, "sir, I am backed clear to the president to guard this shipment being loaded. If you have a question about my loaded gun I suggest you call my battalion commander Col. Irwin and talk to him."

By this time his face was so red I thought he would explode. He instantly wheeled around and off he rushed to I imagined was a phone. I don't know what Col. Irwin told him but I never saw the captain again. The shore patrol left and I went on with my duty of guarding the shipment.

I was on KP at the officers' mess doing the potatoes etc and the soldier I was with asked me if I had seen that nice cake on the counter. I replied that I had not but let's go look. There it was, a beautiful frosted cake just tempting us. We grabbed a knife and cut us each a nice big piece of cake. After that we went back to the storage room to get some sleep on the soft sacks of flour. We were asleep when the mess sergeant found us. He was very angry. He asked us if either one of us knew anything about that cake on the counter. We answered him, "what about it?" He told us that he had baked that special for the officers tonight and someone took a couple of pieces out of it. We looked at him and said, "the cake was very good." He started to cuss us out and threaten all kinds of things that he was going to do to us. We told him to go ahead because we weren't going to be at Fort Hamilton very long. He told us to come with him and led the way to the kitchen. Then he told us that he was going to bake another cake and we could eat the cut cake but we were to leave the newly baked one alone.

We spent many evenings at the USO, United Service Organization. It was a community club in New York City where all service personnel could go to spend a leisure evening relaxing and dancing. The girls that came to dance were not allowed to go out with the service personnel. They could only dance at the USO and socialize.

L to R: Ken Murvine, Greve Machen, Willard Ingraham

Although many of us were farm boys we traveled all over New York City including to the Empire State building, China Town and other sites. In fact, we were surprised when we talked to some of the local people that they had lived in New York City all their lives and had not been out of the city. For us, as soldiers, that was hard to believe that people would get so caught up in their daily life that they were not interested in seeing anything else.

We had eighteen wonderful days enjoying the good food and the many wonders of New York. We explored every night that we could get away from guard or any other duty.

The orders came that we would immediately be shipping out. No one knew where we were going because we were told the captain of our ship and the leader of the convoy would not be opening the orders for our destination until we were one day out to sea. This had to do with the secrecy and security of what had been predetermined.

After we boarded ships and sailed out to sea the last thing we saw on the skyline as we moved further out to sea was the Statue of Liberty on Ellis Island. The Statue of Liberty is located in New York harbor and was a gift of International friendship from the people of France to the people of the United States. It is one of the most universal symbols of political freedom and democracy. The statue of Liberty was dedicated on October 28, 1886 and was designated a national monument on October 15, 1924. The statue was extensively restored in time for her spectacular centennial on July 4, 1986. It struck us with awe, leaving a big lump of sadness in our throats as our ships sailed out of sight of the Statue Of Liberty.

As we were leaving the harbor of New York I saw how dirty the water was. Looking down at the water from the deck of the ship it was impossible to see the fish in the water because it was so dirty it had a muddy green look. After a day travel out to sea I could see that the water started to get a lighter green color. One could still only see fish close to the surface of the water. After two days out to sea the water changed to a blue color and fish could be seen deeper in the water. Also the swells of the ocean began to roll and grow larger in size. It gave me a feeling that the large ship we were on was floating on top of those rolling waves liking to a small bouncing cork in a large pond.

Everyday that we traveled the water was turning to a clean beautiful dark blue. I now felt the enormity of this vast body of water. Nothing was visible except the vast dark blue ocean and the fifty-ship convoy that we were a part of. Our ship was on the right wing of the convoy traveling a zig zag route as we proceeded on our way.

We had previously practiced an emergency drill. Everyone was assigned to one of the life-boats that hung above the side and deck of the ship. We were alerted that a pack of six German submarines were in the area. The captain of the ship's voice came across the loud speaker. He ordered everyone to the top deck with our life jackets on.

Soon we watched in horror as a white streak from a torpedo was headed for the broad side of our ship. In a few seconds we witnessed the superior skill of our captain as he maneuvered the ship fully in a sharp right turn at the precise right moment. We watched as the torpedo barely went along side our ship and continued to go out of sight. The big horns and bells were going off. The noise was deafening and at the same time the sailors were running around the ship like a bunch of ants. It all gave us the excitement of something big going on. We stopped one sailor long enough to ask him what was happening that they were all rushing around. He told us that six German submarines were attacking.

A lot of action was taking place through out the whole convoy. There were two destroyer ships that were in our convoy. We watched them as they sprang into action amongst the ships. They catapulted two planes off their decks and as soon as the planes were airborne they began dropping depth charges all around the convoy of ships, in different places at the same time. At the same time the ships were dropping ash cans that were depth charges. As our ship continued a zig zag pattern and I watched the planes drop the depth charges a thought crossed my mind. The planes had been catapulted off the ship; how were they going to get back on the ship's deck?

As we looked out from the right side of our ship we began to see oil slicks and a small amount of debris floating around on the ocean surface. I began to think about that torpedo and how different our day could have turned out. I am sure most of us on those ships thanked God for having his protective hand over the whole situation that took place. It was definitly a miracle that the torpedo missed our ship. In a different instant with a hit it would have put our ship to the bottom of the ocean.

We were all thankful of the alert and skillful actions of our captain and the sailors as well as the pilots. They saved us all for another day. Some may say it was just the twist of fate but I would say it was the miracle of God's protective hand blessing us. Word was passed down that five of the six German submarines that attacked us that day were destroyed in that battle that day hundreds of miles from anywhere.

On previous convoys there were many troop ships that were sunk by German submarines. It was noted by American intelligence that the Germans had previous knowledge of where the ships would be. All that the German submarines had to do is wait for the convoy to come along. From how swiftly the Germans were receiving these co-ordinance and convoy routes US intelligence knew that some one was sending radio messages to the Germans.

There were thousands of radio broadcasting stations in the US and the questions were, what program, what station, and what person was it? With superb intelligence in play they narrowed it down to one station. Then from one station they needed to know what program could it be coming from and how. Our intelligence finally pin pointed it to the program but then the final question was how was it getting out?

Many of you reading this book will remember that back in the 1940s there was a radio program called Major Bow's Amateur Hour. Major Bows always gave a poem recitation in the beginning or the end of his hour-long program. In those beautiful poems were hidden messages going directly to the submarines from Major Bows radio program. When US intelligence was able to decipher these poems they knew that it was Major Bows.

If the Germans' had been successful in taking over the United States, Major Bows would have been one of the German leaders to govern the US. Many German leaders carried cyanide poison pills on their person that they would swallow rather than be captured.   So it was when US intelligence went to arrest Major Bows he took the cyanide pill.

Ed Sullivan took over the amateur hour program and was the MC of that program for many years after Major Bows.

At the time of our crossing we knew nothing of the Major Bows deception but the rest of the voyage was uneventful except for the many soldiers that got seasick.   On the second or third day out to sea my own stomach was a little upset.   I quickly realized that I needed to eat even though I wasn't hungry.

We had tables that we stood by when we ate our meals aboard ship.   I could not figure out why they had it arranged in this way except perhaps if one got sick while eating one could take off really fast to get to the side rail of the ship.

It was our fifteenth day since leaving the New York Harbor.   We were all getting anxious to walk on land again.   It wasn't long that day though and our ship was docking at the harbor of Swansea, Wales.

CHAPTER: VI
ROSEBUSH

The ship entered the harbor at Swansea, Wales. After docking we were marched a short distance and quartered in nice available houses on the hillside of Swansea. We remained quartered there. Our task in Swansea was to guard the unloading of the secret tanks from the bottom hold of the ship.

One day one of our sergeants was standing on the dock near our ship that was being unloaded. As we approached we could see a seagull sitting on a post in the bay. The sergeant said, "Ingraham, I bet you can't hit that seagull over there on that post." I immediately raised my gun, aimed and bang; no more seagull. The sergeant said, "I didn't think you would shoot."

The next day, I was returning to my quarters after pulling guard and there were three soldiers standing on the sidewalk in front of my quarters in a heated conversation. One of the soldiers was the lieutenant in charge of our group on the ship that we came over on.

Earlier in the day some of my buddies had informed me that the brass was looking for the person that shot the seagull on the dock. It seems that when the shot was heard by some of the local workers that were unloading the ship they had gotten scared and would not come back to work. Anyway when I saw the heated conversation I surmised they were talking about who shot the seagull from on the dock. I walked up to the lieutenant and asked, "sir, I understand you are looking for the person that shot on the dock?" He said, "Yes, do you know who it was?" My answer, "Yes sir, it was me that made that shot." His jaw dropped down leaving him speechless for a moment then he asked, "did you shoot that seagull from the dock?" I answered, "yes sir, it was me." His reply, "go to your quarters and I'll talk to you later." I never did hear a word about the shooting incident after that.

While we were stationed at Swansea we had a few evening passes and attended some dances. It was at these dances that I learned the English dance called The Hokey Pokey. The Welsh girls were very patient in teaching us so it didn't take long to learn the dance. Shortly we were dancing around like all the rest of the dancers. The Welsh girls loved to dance and they were very good at it.

My parents, back home, played for dances all their married life so all of us children had grown up with music.

Many times when we were small we slept on the dance hall benches while they were playing. My father was an old time fiddler and my mother played the piano so we learned how to dance when we were very young. My mother was very patient and had taught us to dance the one step, two step, waltz, polka's, shotish and square dance steps.

We also learned very quickly where we could purchase the well-known fish and chips in Swansea that we all enjoyed. Usually we would start our evenings with fish and chips then go to a pub, which was their tavern, and get one of their dark warm beers. Drinking warm beer did not bother us because we had gotten used to drinking it warm at Camp Bouse, Arizona. The bar tender would kid us by saying, "better drink up boys before your beer gets cold."

When walking down the streets in Swansea I looked for a sign on a store that might be called Ingraham. Because I knew I had a Welsh background. I did find one store sign that did have Ingraham as a name but who knows if there were any relation to my family. I have always said that my heritage was so mixed up I had to be an American. I did know that my ancestory was English, Welsh, Dutch and Norwegian. I have since traced the Ingraham name back to the Mayflower. I found that I was a direct descendent of John Alden, Priscilla Mullins and Captain Miles Standish of the Mayflower.

We continued to guard the unloading of the gizmos at

Swansea using the same security that we had used back in the states. There was a bunch of barrage balloons floating above most of the city and the harbor. The barrage balloons were anchored

71

with ropes and floated in the air at various heights from three hundred to a thousand feet. We asked what the barrage balloons were for and were told that they were there to keep the German planes from flying in low and strafing the installations and the people of the city.

All of us Americans could not get over watching the cars all being driven down the left side of the street. I thought that surely when they came to an intersection I would see one big accident but they seemed to drive in an orderly way following their own standards.

All of the Welsh people were very friendly to all of us American soldiers. They treated us with the highest regard. Sometimes on our nights out we would sample too much of their English beer. As a group, we would walk back to our quarters singing the company A 526th Armored Infantry song. We had made up this song when we rode to Phoenix in the back of an army truck while stationed at Camp Bouse, Arizona.

The song went like this:
We are Captain Michell's raiders
The raiders of the night.
We are dirty S.O.B and we would rather love than fight
IDY-IDY Christ almighty
Who the hell are we
RIP-RAP god dam the armored infantry.

All of us in A company had a good time walking down the middle of the street late at night singing our A company song as well as many other American favorites like Working On the Railroad, Row, Row, Row Your Boat, You Are My Sunshine and many more. By the time we walked back to our quarters singing songs we were all ready for bed.

After the CDL tanks were unloaded from the ship and back in the hands of the respective tank battalion that operated them our guard duty was finished. We listened to a program on the radio that was broadcasting news with Axis Salley from Germany. She broadcasted propaganda to both the English and American soldiers. She would say, "wouldn't it be nice if you were back home now with your girl friend having a good time instead of spending your time over here waiting to get killed?" She spoke perfect English and would rattle on about the luxuries of home that we were all giving up. She tried to make us homesick or tired of training for war but we all laughed and made fun of her nonsense.

Raymond Ingraham
Airforce in Italy

On one mail call I received a letter and a picture of my brother, Raymond. The picture had been taken in his Army Air Force uniform. He told me that he was to ship out to Italy soon. Now all three boys from our family were in the army.

After completing our work at Swansea we were all feeling good about the time we had spent here. We had many happy memories of the people of Swansea and their kindness that they shared with us. Our orders were to prepare for a move that we had known was coming. We headed for a little town called Rosebush. We did not go into the town of Rosebush but near by in a green sheep pasture. After our arrival it did not take A company of the 526 A.I.B. long to install the pyramidal tents and our army camp was in place. Our tents were set up in a big field of green. It was like having our own private lawn.

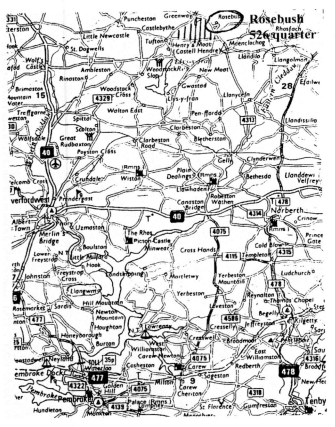

Once again we had our regular morning roll call then we were told to line up for our exercises. We would also march out about three miles from camp and up a big hill to perform field problems for the day. One day after getting to the location, Lt. Willyard needed a runner to take a message back to camp and return with an answer. He gave an order, "send me Ingraham", that way he will be too tired to write letters tonight and I won't have to spend my time censoring them."

All of our letters were still being censored and were all the rest of the time that we were in the army. I realized that I needed to write a lot of letters to receive letters. I was fortunate, I always received many letters from friends and relatives back home as well as from many of my friends that were in the service somewhere else. Some of my buddies had overheard the lieutenant ask for me for the runner mission and told me what he had said about my letter writing. Lt. Willyard's reasoning did not work because I was behind on my letter writing so that night I kicked out five long letters.

While we were over seas the letters from home seemed more important than ever. I felt sorry for the soldiers that seldom received a letter at mail call.

It was May of 1944 and the days seemed to be getting longer all the time. In fact, at eleven thirty at night it was still very light out. My mother had told me about the land of the mid-night sun in Norway but I did not realize that this area of Great Britain would be affected.

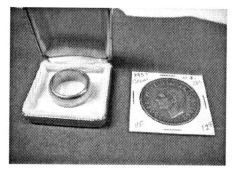

I had a lot of time in the evenings and would go down to the railroad tracks just below our camp. I decided to make a ring from an English Crown coin. The coin was about the size of a fifty-cent piece and almost 100 percent silver. I used a rock and pounded the coin using the track of the railroad as my anvil. After I pounded the coin wide enough to punch a hole in it I filed it until I got the finger size and the width I wanted. After pounding the coin into a ring I wore it for the remaining time I was in the service. I still have that ring to this day.

My mother sent me a small bible when I was in Swansea. I carried it in my breast pocket all the time. The bible gave me great comfort by just carrying it. It gave me the feeling of God always being close to me and having his protective hand over me.

Cookies were sent from home that I always enjoyed. The people at the post office back home had told my mother that if she was sending cookies over seas they should be sent in a tin container. Mother baked up a big tin container of my favorite filled cookies that she knew I really liked and sent them. About three weeks later when they arrived I opened the container of cookies and found that they were all moldy. I did not let them go to waste because I knew a little mold would not hurt any ones health. My buddies and I just peeled the mold off and ate the cookie. I did write my mother though and asked her not to send filled cookies in a tin container.

As to the fog in the British Isles, I am sure there is no place in the world that can equal the denseness of that fog. Needless to say, every thing shut down when the fog set in because, I am telling you the truth when I say that you could not see your hand before your face. We had to walk across the green field to get to our mess tent and get into the chow line to get our food. Walking over there in the fog we bumped into someone before we even knew they were close to us. We found the safest way to get to the mess tent was to talk to a buddy as we walked together. We could be heard talking, before we otherwise collided into some one.

For those at home, it would have been beyond any imagination to have seen all of the American equipment and soldiers every where on the British Isles. There were so much men and equipment everywhere we traveled that we often made jokes. "There is so much American equipment scattered around this island I am sure it is about to sink."

The days were now all cloudy and we had rainy weather, rather nasty, as the English would say. The day that all of us had been anticipating arrived. It was June 6, 1944 and D-Day as it was known. D –Day meaning departure day.

"At ease." General Eisenhower talks with weary GIs.

It had been in January 1944 that General Eisenhower had arrived in England to take supreme command of all the allied forces. By March the eight and ninth US Air Force and the English Royal Air Force started a three-month continuous bombing of targets along the coast and northern France and Western Germany.

The Germans knew that an invasion was coming but they weren't sure when or where it would take place. D-Day was planned for June 5th but because of bad weather it was post poned for twenty-four hours.

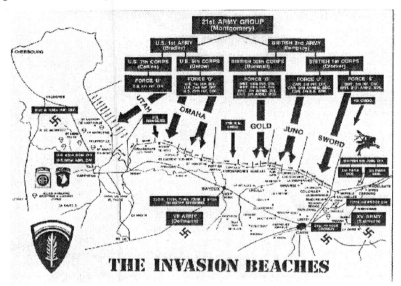

THE INVASION BEACHES

On June 6th four thousand ships landed on the Omaha and Utah beachheads plus three other beaches all along the coast of France that the English landed on all at split second timing. All across the English Channel battleships, cruisers and destroyers guarded the flanks of the armada of ships. An umbrella of airplanes covered in case the German planes or submarines would show up. The battle ships laid down a barrage of shells on the entrenched Germans in pillboxes that were scattered all along the coastal area. At the same time all of this was going on the landing crafts, the LCIIPS and LCMS all loaded with infantry soldiers, headed into the beaches of Omaha, Utah and the other three beaches. At the end of the first twenty-four hours sixty six thousand troops had landed on the two beaches. In seven days two hundred and fifty thousand Americans were on shore in France.

While all of this was going on a large force of paratroopers were parachuting back of the German lines and establishing a control point amongst the hedgerows of France. Also ahead of the armada of ships the minesweepers were already clearing all the landing area and marking it as cleared for the landing crafts that soon followed the minesweepers.

The weather was terrible at that time and stopped many planes from bombing and strafing the many gun emplacements the Germans had strung all along the whole coast line.

The beachhead secured, Allied reinforcements come ashore.

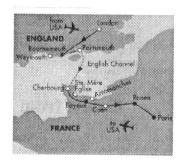

Cherbourg Harbor, directly across the water from England, was very well fortified by the Germans. It was a very important harbor for the Allied forces to control for a direct supply line. A frontal attack on Cherbourg would have cost too many soldiers lives. Once the Omaha and Utah beach heads were well established and paratroopers establishing their area further inland the Americans cut the Cherbourg peninsula completely off. They struck the well-fortified Cherbourg from behind. It wasn't long that the Germans saw they were overpowered and surrendered. With the supply line shortened the Allied forces pushed harder into France on the way to Germany.

Back in Rosebush we were told that in the first three days of D-Day there were eighteen thousand dead that was picked up at Omaha and Utah beachheads. Rumors had it that we were on alert but no move out orders came. Later we heard that the invasion had gone better than anticipated. Everything was on wait and see how the invasion front went. We kept training in our shooting skills etc. while waiting for further orders.

The scuttlebutt had it that it would be soon that we would be going to France. We were told we would be landing on the place of the now famous invasion of the Utah beachhead that had already been secured. Allied forces were already on their way into France. In August our orders came; we were to move out to go to France.

CHAPTER: VII

NORMANDY

We had our orders and it was time for the 526 A.I.B. to prepare to move. In early morning of the seventeenth of August, 1944 we left our tent camp at Rosebush, Wales. We traveled all day and by late afternoon arrived at the port of Swansea, Wales.

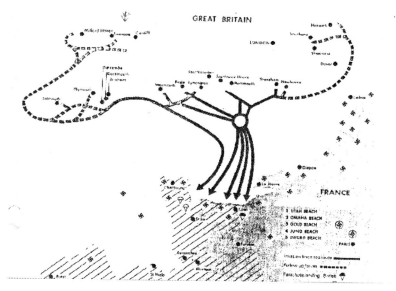

The next day we boarded our landing craft troop ships and were on our way to cross the English Channel. We were heading for the European continent and the Utah beachhead of France. This was one of the beachheads used on D-Day, during that now famous invasion day. The arrow map shows the five landing sites of that D-Day invasion. Left to right is, 1 Utah Beach, 2 Omaha Beach, 3, Gold Beach, 4, Juno Beach and 5 Sword beach. The British and Canadian troops landed on Number three, four and five beaches on D-Day.

The landing crafts that we were on had big metal boxes with open tops with trap doors that opened up in the front end of the boat. I must tell you that sailing across the English Channel in the choppy water of the channel in open boats was not very much fun. I estimate the English Channel was about thirty miles across.

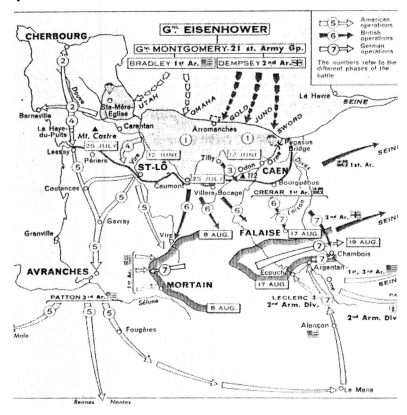

We talked to the grey haired pilot of our boat and he told us that he was involved in transporting the troops to shore on the D-Day invasion. He asked us, "do you see my white hair? Well, my hair was dark brown before the invasion but you can see the color is now white. I am twenty-eight years old and look like an old man. But, I will tell you at that time my hair turned white practically over night."

The 526th lands in France

There were hundreds of half sunken ships still in the channel scattered everywhere. When we arrived at the Utah beach the landing crafts could not go all the way to shore so we had to jump off and walk in water above our knees to get to shore. Our landing was at Utah Beach and from here we were to leave for St. Germain, France.

We stayed on the beach for a short time then moved on to Granville, Normandy, France where we were assigned to the 10th armored group. They were located in an apple orchard and we joined up with them there. It was raining hard and everything was muddy. It was like clay gumbo when we walked in it. The mud balled up on our shoes making things miserable. Not only that we had to pitch our little pup tents and live with it.

St. Pair and Granville were close to our camp. On our free time we were able to go to these small towns and enjoy

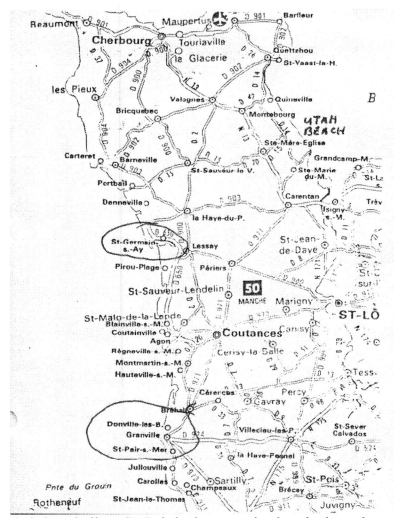

their hospitality. St. Pair had a very nice beach along the ocean so when we got some time off it was nice to make use of their beach. Some of the soldiers picked up some souvenirs around this area. How they got some of these souvenirs is their own story to tell. I do have a picture of some of the 526 Armored Battalion soldiers that acquired a German Swastika flag that is in a photo in this chapter.

84

L to R: Boyce Williams, John Sankey, Charles Crumpton, David Lowe, Jerome Stapp, Richard Clark, and John Kalisek (APPLE ORCHARD, NORMANDY)   A Company, 1944

Lt Willyard kept us in physical shape by giving us special exercise training. He lined us up near one of the 526 A.I.B. halftracks and we took turns crawling up on top of the fifty calbre gun enclosure on the halftrack. Then we jumped off that halftrack carrying our MI Garand rifle. Lt. Willyard said, "when you land you hold your gun in both hands, relax and roll as you land." I don't know how the rest of the soldiers faired in the jump but I relaxed as he had said and rolled with the landing. I apparently twisted my back as I landed. It left me with a very sore back for about three days but I never told anyone about it. I am sure some of the other jumpers did the same thing.

There were some pill-boxes on the coast line of France that was just a few miles from our camp that we wanted to check out. The pill-boxes were concrete gun emplacements that the German army used for their coast line defense. There was about a dozen of us riding two half-tracks that went to see if the pill-boxes were no longer in use. As we approached the area the half-tracks were parked and we started walking across

85

a field in a clearing. The pill-boxes were about a quarter of a mile across the field.

JOHN F. SANKEY

We walked about half way across the field when we discovered we were in the middle of a mine-field. Looking around we soon discovered a personnel mine with its three prong metal points sticking out of the ground about one inch. We identified it as a personnel mine called "the bouncing betty." When the prongs of the mine were disturbed or the strings scattered on the ground that were attached to the prongs then the mine would be triggered. The bouncing betty would fly up out of the ground about four foot high then explode possibly killing anyone in close range of the explosion. The mines were full of sharp metal parts that were intended to do a mass amount of damage to the intruders.

We all had minimum amount of training to disarm these land mines. They were very tricky to disarm once set because anyone of those wires that were attached to the mine if not found and cleared could set the mine off. I was going to try to disarm it but my buddies said, "no, just mark the spot and leave it alone."

We continued walking across the field very carefully to the pill-boxes and checked them out. Afterward we picked our way back out of there without getting blown up. Back at the half-tracks we all mounted into the half-tracks except S/Sgt Raymond Dykes who stood on the running board of the half-track watching for possible mines in our path. We had just turned the half-track around and started to move forward when a land mine blew up. It knocked out one track of the half – track and at the same time S/Sgt Raymond Dykes was blown off the half-track landing a few feet away from the half-track. He was all right, not seriously injured, but very much in a daze for a while. The rest of us inside the half-track were all right and none of us injured other than shaken up.

Back at camp we went to pick up our usual meal which was one can of whatever; beans, hash or maybe spaghetti with four cigarettes on the top of the can. The cigarettes were always some strange brand that was unrecognizable to us like Chelse or some other name just as meaningless. These were the only cigarettes we received since our arrival in France with our one can of C rations.

One day Bill Rogers and I were able to get a box of K rations. We thought we were really living up town as we proceeded to eat the contents of the box of K rations. This was the first time I knew that K rations as food was given to some in the army. I would say that the K rations were very tasty and there was an assortment of different types of food in that box. Needless to say, Bill and I had at least one good meal that day.

St. Pair   beach

St Pair

St. Pair was always a fun place to visit because of their nice sandy beaches along the coastline. The people in St. Pair were very friendly and welcomed all of us openly.

View of St. Pair

While we were camped in the apple orchard near Granville, France we had the good fortune of visiting one of the Seven Wonders of the World, Mount Saint Michel, off the coast of France. It is located just a few miles from Granville

Mount Saint Michel

and one of the most picturesque castles that I have ever seen. The castle is located on a large rock formation about a mile off

89

St. Michel

the coast of France. When the tide was in the castle was completely surrounded by water except the causeway that had a road leading from the mainland to the castle. The tide was out when we visited the castle so they let us take our shoes off and we walked from the mainland across the open area of sand. This area would have been completely covered with water when the tide came in. It was about a mile walk across to the castle taking the route we did.

Mount Saint Michel left an indelible memory on me with its setting that was so richly steeped in history and so perfect in architecture. Another spectacle was the flooding at particularly high tides around the island twice a month at new and full moon and in a greater force at the spring equinox.

The abbey's origin goes back to the beginning of the eighth century when the arch-angel Michael appeared before Aubert, Bishop of Avranches who founded an oratory on the island known as Mount Tombe. This was replaced and renamed Mount St. Michel first by Carolingian Abbey and then until the sixteenth century by a series of Romanseque and

Gothic churches. Each was more splendid than its predecessor. The abbey was fortified but never captured.

St. Michel – Tide out

The construction was a masterpiece of skill. The granite blocks had to be brought from either the Chausey Islands or Brittany and hauled up to the site which at its crest was so narrow that supports had to be built up from the rocks below. People flocked to the Mount even during the hundred-year war. The English who held the surrounding region granted safe passage with payment to the faithful nobles. Rich merchants and beggars who were given free shelter by the monks all flocked to the great almshouse. Hoteliers and souvenir craftsmen prospered even then. People bought emblems bearing the effigy of St. Michael and lead caskets were filled with sand from the beach.

Crossing the bay had its perils and there were deaths among the multitudes of people from drowning and sinking into the quicksand. The mount became known as St. Michael in peril from the sea.

View of Abbey

Inside Abbey

There were stages in the abbeys construction. The Romanesque abbey (11 and 12 century) between 1017 and 1144 a church was built on the mounts summit utilizing the earlier Carolingian building as a crypt. Our lady below ground, Notre Dame, Sous Terre and as support for the platform on which to stand the three final bags of the Romanesque nave. Additional crypts were built on which to support the transepts and the chancel that extended beyond the rock crest. The conventual's buildings were constructed on the mounts west slope and on either side of the name.

The abbey declined into a commandeer and discipline among the monks became lax under this system. Abbots were not necessarily churchmen and did not always supervise the abbey although they took the stipends. In the seventeenth century the Marists were charged with reforming the monastery but in fact only made superficial architectural changes.

The conversion of the abbey into a prison in the late eighteen and early nineteenth century brought it even lower. The museums evoked complacent scenes of horror from this period. In 1874 the abbey and ramparts passed into the care of the state, which restored them considerably.

One of many rooms

On our visit we observed many well structured rooms in the castle. I won't say that we saw all of the rooms there because there were too many rooms to visit in the time we had to spend. We did go from top to bottom of this large castle. We went down into the dungeon below the castle where the smell was musty and very unclean. It gave us a feeling of sadness and a sense that many hardships and sadness had taken place down there. I was glad to get out of that area because of the terrible feeling that came over me while I was there.

Wheel in cupola

A couple of my buddies and I decided to see what this castle had to offer at the top. After a long climb we found ourselves as far as we could go but looking out the open windows on the top we could see that there was another little space up in the cupola. We had to find out what was up there so we climbed out on the roof. By standing on the peak of the roof we could look into that small space but what we thought we would see was not there. We were sure that we would find an old bell up there but to our surprise there was a big wheel with a rope on it. Now what do you suppose that big round wooden wheel was doing up there? We just had to find out so we climbed up through those windows on top and entered to take a good look. Then we knew what the wheel was all about. Under that big wooden wheel was a shaft going down to the ground floor of the castle. This was the secret of how they were able to lift all those heavy blocks to the top level of the castle while they were constructing this part. They would have used one, two or maybe three slaves inside of the wheel. By human power the slaves would have walked inside of the wheel pulling up the heavy loads that were attached by the rope up to the top level.

Observing all of this only arose our curiosity. We crawled into the big wooden wheel and started walking around inside the wheel. That wasn't good enough so we started to run around inside that big wheel to see what it would do in high speed. It was great fun but finally we decided we had enough. We climbed out the window, down the roof and back into the castle. By the time we got back down to ground level everyone of the soldiers were getting ready to leave.

While we had been looking the castle over trucks had been brought around to the other side of the castle where there was a road to shore. We all loaded up in the trucks and relaxed and talked about the different things we had discovered in this

Granville

95

castle as we headed for camp. I am sure the old castle could tell all of us stories that would stretch the imagination of everyone. On our way back to camp the truck took us through Granville, France that was about thirty miles from St. Mount Michel. All of us considered this had been a very good day touring the quaint castle and broke the every day routine from training.

Granville beach

Prime minister Winston Churchill of England offered the CDL (Canal Defense Lights) tanks on his and Eisenhower's top-secret communication between the two leaders. In October, 1944, apparently, Churchill offered a regiment of the tanks to Eisenhower. He told Eisenhower that Field Marshall Sir Harold Alexander wanted them in Italy but was offering them to Eisenhower because he was the top bull.

Eisenhower wrote that he appreciated Churchill's offer of the tanks but thorough study had revealed that shipping and special training problems could not be resolved in time for that formation to be of great value to us during the period in which decisive operations were feasible due to the weather. He suggested that Churchill furnish reinforcements to Montgomery.

I think that was a wise decision that Eisenhower made because, my personal opinion, the CDL's would not have worked effectively in the terrain of Normandy due to all the hedge-rows involved. I am sure that the communications between the two big leaders of Allied Forces is the reason the 526 A.I.B. never went to battle with the use of CDLs.

St. Pair-sur-Mer

St. Pair-sur-Mer

In October of 1944 the 526 Armored Infantry Battalion received orders to prepare to move to Verdun, France. All of us in the 526th had been in that apple orchard living in those pup tents for a long time and very much needed a shower. In Verdun the army brought in an open shower truck that had about a dozen shower heads on each side of the back of the truck with a tent separation to both sides but open to the world on the shower side except for a five foot canvas in front of all the shower heads looking outside.

They lined us up to a tent before going up onto the truck bed. We stripped off all our clothes and each of us took a turn going through the showers. At the other end we went into a tent where we were issued a change of clean clothes.

CHAPTER VIII
TASK FORCE COUNTER INTELLEGENCE

In October, 1944 orders came in to the battalion to move to Verdun, France and become a part of Special Troops Of 12th Army Group. From Verdun the 526 Armored Infantry Battalion departed for destinations in Belgium and Luxembourg. Company C 526 Armored Infantry Battalion was designated as a guard company for Eagle TAC. The remainder of the battalion was employed by T force, 12th Army Group.

From The 30th of October to The 17th of December 1944 C Company was permanently stationed with the headquarters at Harze, Belgium. It was there that company C trained for their mission with T force. The training consisted of hand-to-hand combat, intelligence, searching prisoners, dealing with civilians, learning the German language and fighting in cities. A few problems were held in street fighting among the ruins in Liege.

It must be understood that the 526 Armored Infantry Battalion holds the distinction of being the only separate armored infantry battalion in the army that worked with the T Force of the 12th army group as Special Troops. The 526th Armored Infantry Battalion would often work separately by companies. Yes, also sometimes as individual squad units in order to reach our objectives and missions assigned to us.

At the outset of operations on continental Europe it was realized in the higher intelligence echelons of the theater that existing organic intelligence agencies would be inadequate to the mission for exploiting fully the larger and more important cities and areas containing intelligence and counter intelligence targets. It was therefore decided at supreme headquarters Allied Expeditionary Force to organize collecting units known

99

as T Force that was designed to operate at army group level. Their mission was seizing, safeguarding and facilitating the exploitation of important intelligence and counter intelligence targets in the larger cities and in designated areas that were uncovered in the course of the advance of the Allied forces across Europe.

The initial planning for the employment of T Force in the European theater of operations was undertaken under the direction of Supreme Headquarters, Allied expeditionary force in June and July of 1944. Colonel Francis P. Tompkins was designated as officer of G-2 section headquarters 12th army group responsible for the handling of T force matters on August 1944.

Following the new assignment T force headquarters moved to Spa, Belgium where the balance of the allowed grades and ratings joined the headquarters to complete staff. In addition, there were readjustments made in the intelligence specialist teams attached to the force.

After additional forces moved into the vicinity of Remouchamps in Belgium the force was reinforced by the permanent attachment of the 526th Armored Infantry Battalion (less company C) under the command of Lieutenant Colonel Carlisle B. Irwin on October 1944. During the months of October, November and December organization of the headquarters and the force was

Son Writes From Belgium

The following letter was received recently by Mr. and Mrs. Lyle Ingraham from their son Willard:

Belgium, Oct. 31, 1944.

Dearest Mother and Dad:

It has been about two weeks since I've heard from you or anyone but I know it has been no fault of yours.

I was at Verdun a couple of days; it's one of the biggest cities in France I do imagine.

I thought that the oxen working days were over but I have seen a lot of them working in fields in place of horses—and at one place I saw them working a horse and an ox together on a walking plow; it seems so strange to see four oxen hooked up to a drag on various other machinery. It's surprising the funny little things we see—a lot of things that make us laugh our insides out, but to the people here it's an every day event. And then again there are places you pass that strike you with their beauty.

Here in Belgium it's mostly covered with pine and pretty trees. I know one thing if I get back I'll never forget what I've seen over here. Around here it's a pretty good hunting district—in more ways than one. But they do have deer—wild boars, etc.

Don't worry as I'll be all right.

100

completed with the addition of necessary signal communications personnel and the semi-permanent attachments of various intelligence detachments and units.

With the staffing complete headquarters entered upon two important programs. The first was the preparation of target materials for the cities that had been designated as T force areas of operation in the future. Namely they were Cologne, Bonn, Coblenz, Frankfurt, Wiesbaden, Karlsruhe and Mannheim.

The second program was for the purpose of training assigned and attached personnel in the organization and method of operation of T force to increase efficiency. After preliminary orientation of all units an extended training program was entered upon to prepare the force, as it was then constituted, for T force type operations. This included preliminary indoctrination command post exercises and field exercises employing troops using as a training area the bombed out portions of Liege, Belgium.

Emphasis was placed upon the special problems arising with the possibility of mines and booby traps, the necessity for constant communication preparation of a signal operations instructions and the formulation of a working vocabulary.

American World War I
Soldiers at Liege, Belgium

Before leaving Verdun, France, A company of the 526 Armored Infantry Battalion viewed the huge cemetery located there that held thousands of AmericanWWI soldiers. The cemetery was nicely kept and it was a very striking view to see all of those white crosses spread over acres of ground.

Buzz Bomb

The 526 Armored Infantry Battalion was headed for Liege, Belgium. We had just entered the city of Liege when we saw a buzz bomb coming toward our direction. It was a buzz bomb that was a flying bomb that the Germans launched for, I think, more for psychological reasons rather than for effective damage. Although when the bomb landed it left a big hole in the ground.

When the Germans launched the bomb they put the calculated target amount of gas into the tank for the motor that propelled the bomb. Supposedly the bomb would drop when the tank was out of gas. We heard that these bombs, at times, would sputter before dropping, therefore, ruining the accuracy. When we heard the buzz bomb coming it sounded like an old Model T Ford car. As the buzz bomb approached we all fired at it and then, "oh no," here it comes down on us.

The bomb landed on the other side of the buildings where we were parked. It landed in an open area and no damage was done to any of the buildings and no one was hurt. The explosion may have shattered some windows in buildings close by but there was no structural damage that was visible. I have inserted a picture of a buzz bomb in this chapter.

After our experience in Liege, Belgium with the buzz bomb we proceeded through Belgium. In this area there was more timber country. It was more like the western part of my own state in western Washington except the trees were smaller and more scattered.

We had noted coming through France and Belgium, no matter where we went, we saw writings "Kilroy was here." We found the writings on the walls of many buildings, public structures, on logs on beaches, latrines and any other place you could imagine writing. We knew why the writings, "Kilroy was here," because from the coast of France on through any place the American army had been soldiers left the well known written phrase.

When we saw the writings we always added another "Kilroy was here", in the same area. Just think, with all of the American soldiers in that European theater of operations and many adding another "Kilroy was here," no space was missed. Writings were on top of flag poles, in subways, on bridges, in shipyards and army camps. The British exploring passageways inside of the Great Pyramid found writing on the ancient walls, "Kilroy was here."

Joseph Stalin exiting the men's room during World War II at the Yalta conference said to his interpreter, "find out who this Kilroy is."

Our force ended up Chateau Grimonster, the Barons mansion named for the owner, Baron Descamps. Inserted is a picture of Chateau Grimonster as it looked in 1944 with the owner's signature on it.

The chateau had many rooms that housed the A company of 526 Armored Infantry very adequately. That was our home from October to December 17th, 1944.

After we got settled in our new quarters we began training on two important programs. The first was the preparation of target material for the cities that had been designated as T force areas of operation in the future. It was like it had been for the German cities of Cologne, Bonn, Coblenz, Frankfurt, Wiesbaden, Karlsruhe and Mannheim.

Our 526 Armored Infantry was not only working with T force, (task force), but also with counter intelligence called CIC (Counter Intelligence Corp). We met Lt. Oppenhiemer of the CIC. He taught us many ways that we could subdue our target people and search them while they remained under our control. He also taught us to beware of many different types of booby traps. He gave examples of favorite tricks as in an office building they would leave a desk drawer barely open showing a pistol inside. If the desk drawer was opened wider an explosion was detonated killing anyone near. The German's were aware of the American hunt for souvenirs, especially pistols.

Most offices and big public rooms had most certainly a big picture of Hitler hanging on the wall. When we saw these big pictures of Hitler we would use the first thing handy and throw it at the picture and smashing it to pieces. Other times we would just shoot the picture off the wall. The Germans became aware of our actions so they began booby trapping the pictures.

We soon found ways of getting rid of those charges. The desk drawer booby traps were ones that we tied a string around the desk pull handle, then went outside and yanked the drawer open. Lt Oppenhiemer also taught us an awareness of the kind of targets we would be looking for like German officers etc.

We also had to be aware of going up steps into an office building. Especially the second step up if the steps were wooden. Many times the Germans would loosen the second step and install a plunger type device under the step. If that step was stepped on it would ignite a powerful charge under it. Anyone stepping on this booby trap would certainly be killed.

Besides the work with counter intelligence we worked with the T force, standing guard at many vital places to keep looters out or prevent damage to many of those buildings deemed important. Emphasis was continually placed on the special problems arising from possibilities of mines and booby traps. Also there was the necessity for constant communication, instructions and to formulate a working German vocabulary.

One day three of us at the Chateau Grimonster were standing near the back door of the building when we heard a whishing sound and an immediate plop. A reserve gas tank from a P40 fighter plane had hit about fifteen feet from where the three of us were standing. It was usual for planes to drop their spare gas tanks when they went dry. I would make you a bet that pilot was trying to hit the chateau when he released that gas tank.

Another time we saw a fighter plane coming into a field near us with a dead stick, (meaning with no motor running or a forced landing.) The pilot did a superb job of setting that plane down in the middle of that field with no damage to his plane. He got out, after landing and looked all around to see where he was and then he saw us standing by the chateau. We motioned for him to come over. I am sure that he was happy to see that he was in friendly territory. As he approached us he told us he was headed for his home base and simply ran out of gas.

Lt Willyard continued to teach us hand to hand combat and also about explosives. He showed us how we could use the TNT blocks, primer cord and a cap and then we could blow anything we wanted using the formulas he gave us. One day a buddy of mine and I decided we would try out the formulas. We looked around and saw a big pine tree about eighteen inches in diameter and about fifty foot tall standing maybe five hundred feet out in front of the chateau. We applied the formula taking into consideration where we wanted the tree to fall and how many blocks of TNT we would use as well as the TNT wrapped with primer cord on the tree. Then we calculated how long a primer cord was needed to lay out from the tree so we could light it and get away safely. After we checked and double checked it was time to install the dynamite cap to the primer cord. I did not have a tool to crimp the dynamite cap onto the primer cord so I did what came naturally. I used my teeth to crimp the dynamite cap onto the primer cord.

We calculated that everything was correctly done, lighted the fuse and yell, "fire in the hole." We ran back away for safety and watched as that big tree folded over and landed at exactly the spot we wanted it to land.

We did get a few passes to go into Liege, Belgium while at the chateau. One time while in Liege a bunch of us A company of 526 decided to go to a big indoor swimming pool. The pool was enclosed with all glass panes over the pool area. Around the pool, on all sides, there were three stories with rooms with balconies overlooking the pool. On one side of the pool there were open taverns on each floor that faced out to the entrance to the balconies with chairs and tables on the balconies where people sat and drank while they visited and watched the activities in the pool area.

I challenged Bill Rogers that if he would dive off the springboard on the third floor that I would do the same. He said that I should go first. Up I went to the third floor through the tavern and out the door to the balcony and onto the spring board above the swimming pool. When I stepped out onto the springboard I was thinking. "What did I get myself into?" I had never in my life ever dove off a springboard that was this high before. Looking down it was a long way down. Then again we had been drinking so at that time it was making me feel pretty brave. I looked down again, drew in a deep breath and jumped on the springboard and down I went head-first.

As I crawled out of the pool I told Bill Rogers it was his turn. He said, "no, I don't think so." With a little coaxing he went up to the third floor to the springboard and jumped feet first. When he came out of the pool I reminded him we had agreed to go head first off that spring board but he insisted he would not do that. I told him I would take his turn and back up I went to the third floor and made another dive. One thought did cross my mind while I was in that swimming pool and that was, "what if a buzz bomb landed close to the pool area? It would not be the place to be with so much glass overhead.

Back at the chateau Lt. Oppinheimer brought specialists in to teach us the German language. We were to learn at least the command part of the language so we could tell our prisoners what they were supposed to do.

My squad was Hq squad of 2nd platoon of A company 526 A.I.B. When S/Sgt Gribble was not available I served as acting squad leader. One day I was given a mission to take my squad five miles from Chateau Grimonster and search for possible German paratroopers that may have dropped in our vicinity. As a squad we searched at least five miles for anything that moved but found nothing that looked suspicious to us so we stopped for a cigarette break. Someone had a camera with them and took a picture of my squad that I have

Fr R: L to R: Kenneth Murvine, FrankDavis,
Jack Stredwick, Willard Ingraham
Bk R: L to R: Elmer Reaves, Russell Nichols,
Henry Little, Cleve Collins

placed on following page.

On December 17, 1944 we received orders that we would all move out of the Chateau Grimonster within three hours and would not be coming back.

CHAPTER IX
BATTLE OF THE BULGE

Hitler's army took terrible losses on D-Day along the Omaha and Utah beaches of France. The Allied forces continued to push the German army back through the hedgerows of France. The German fighting force through Normandy was taking a beating until Hitler's army decided to pull back closer to Germany and form a new line of defense. This gave the Allied forces a chance to make larger gains in their push to Germany.

Germans on the move

Hitler had a last ditch plan that would put Germany in control again. The plan was to use the 1st and 2nd SS Panzer Division led by Col Jochen Peiper that were the crack troops of Hitler's army to break through the Allied defense line at Stavelot and Malmedy. Within a forty-eight hour strike they would move on through Leige, Belgium on their way to Antwerp, Belgium where the British army was in control and push the British off the European continent.

Hitler reasoned, with the British army out of the way and controlled, the American army would weaken to the point the Germans could then concentrate on the Russians to get them to come to a negotiated settlement. This push came to be known as the battle of The Belgian Bulge. Col. Jochen Peiper moved his thrust to initiate Hitler's plan.

As a young commander, Col. Jochen Peiper had earned a reputation with his thrust through France and Russia. Hitler wanted this crack unit to lead this most important mission to break through the American defenses then a fast thrust on the coast at Antwerp, Belgian.

He led his 1st and 2nd SS Panzer divisions toward Malmedy with his armored column of tanks, half- tracks and German soldiers that spread back for fifteen miles.

At the same time on the morning of the seventeenth of December an American unit, B Company 285th Field Artillary observation battalion with 86 soldiers headed toward Baugnez Crossroad which was located on the north side of the Ambleve river. A group of Germans were closing in on the American unit and began firing.

Col. Jochen Peiper brought in his column up the South side of the Ambleve river and headed north to Stavelot. Lt. Lary observed the overwhelming German force that they were facing. He immediately threw up his hands and ordered his group to surrender. The Germans brought up some tanks and ordered this American group to follow their convoy for a short distance. When they got back to Baugnez Crossroad the Germans ordered their prisoners out into a field. They brought up machine guns and the killing commenced.

The Germans massacred all eight-six of their prisoners in that field at Baugnez Crossroad. After the massacre some Germans walked among the bodies to see if anyone was still alive and if they observed any body movement they shot the body in the head. The Germans stayed for a short time to make sure all of the Americans were dead and satisfied themselves that their dirty work was accomplished then they left.

Malmedy Massacre

Unknown to the German assassins there were eight American soldiers that were bloody and wounded playing dead until the Germans left the area. These eight soldiers made their way back to the American lines with difficulty. They made their escape to freedom as they crawled away badly wounded not knowing where they might meet up with German soldiers again. These brave men had their own story to tell. The acting battery commander of the 285th Field Observation Battalion B company who surrendered his unit over to the Germans that fatal morning survived and told the whole story of that atrocity.

.

The Germans continued heading north toward Stavelot on the south side of the Ambleve river. When they came to the cross road to Malmedy Col. Jochen Peoper was sure that the 12th Panzer Division had that area all under control so he bypassed Malmedy and continued on hoping to cover the twenty more miles to Stavelot by night fall which was then the seventeenth of December. Malmedy and Stavelot were both located on the north side of the Ambleve river. At Stavelot he planned to organize his big fighting force to proceed the next morning on the eighteenth and begin his big push across the Ambleve River into Stavelot and on to the big push to Antwerp, Belgium.

Germans on the move

Col. Jochen Peiper was known to take captured American prisoners and make them dig graves for dead German soldiers. Afterwards he killed the grave diggers.

Col. Jochen Peiper's plan after arriving at Stavelot was to get ready to break through the American defense line in Stavelot and get all of his vehicles across the bridge to the north side at the Ambleve River. He would then go through Stavelot and capture the bridges across the Meuse river south of Liege, Belgium and move on to his goal, Antwerp, Belgium.

Col. Jochen Peiper had been pushing his army hard for the last three days. He knew his force of over four thousand five hundred soldiers and ninety tanks needed a well deserved rest before pushing on another seven days before he would reach his goal. His plan was to start his big push the next

Germans on the move

morning on the 18th of December, 1944 at five in the morning then cross the bridge over to the north side of the Ambleve river into Stavelot. To accomplish this he had to break the American defense line at Stavelot.

Going back to that same day in the morning of December seventeenth, 1944 Col. Carlisle Irwin Battalion commander of the 526 Armored Infantry Battalion alerted the battalion for combat duty. The companys were to proceed as follows.

Headquarters Company with Captain Robert Corts as company commander, quartered in Hartze, Belgium was to take his company to Stavelot, Belgium and make contact with Major Solis, Executive Officer of T Force who would be in command of the Stavelot operation.

A Company with Captain Charles Mitchell as company commander quartered at Chateau Grimonster near Liege, Belgium was to take one platoon of 825 T.D. Battalion to Stavelot with him. He was to make contact with Major Solis at Stavelot.

. The 526th Armored Infantry Battalion had three hours to pack up and leave Chateau Grimonster where company A had been staying the past few months and would not be returning. The word was that some German paratroopers had landed near Stavelot, Belgium. The 526th was to go clean them out and set up a defensive position at Stavelot.

B Company 526 Armored Infantry Battalion with Captain Richard Wessel as company commander quartered at Comblain La-Tour, Belgium was to meet A company 825 T.D. Battalion in LaReid, Belgium and join up with company B. They then would join to the 99th (Norwegian) infantry battalion at Remouchamps, Belgium and proceed to Malmedy, Belgium by way of Spa, Belgium.

Before entering Malmedy the column was met by guides from the 291st Engr. Battalion who led the column into Malmedy. By that time the 99th Infantry had arrived and the BTN Co (Battalion commanding officer) of the 99th was placed in command and given orders to plan the defense.

All three companys of the 526 Armored Infantry Battalion prior to the 17th of December, 1944 were quartered within a ten mile area of each other.

A Company 526 Armored Infantry moved out with the strength of about 250 men as was the strength in numbers of men in each of the other companys of the 526 A.I.B. Little did the 526 Armored Infantry Battalion realize that they were headed for the biggest battle they would ever encounter. They traveled most of that very cold and very dark night to get to Stavelot. They rode in open half-tracks.

My squad was Headquarters Squad of the Second Platoon of A Company 526 Armored Infantry Battalion with Lt. Willyard as our platoon leader Jack Stredwick was our half-track driver. He drove all the way with the half-track slit lights from a little headlight that gave out not much more light than a lightning bug because of security reasons.

As we all traveled from Liege, Belguim to our destination in Stavelot we discovered that some of the road signs had been changed to go a different direction. It was discovered soon enough to correct any mishap that might have happened. We stayed on coarse and arrived at Stavelot about two thirty A.M. in the morning of the eighteenth of December.

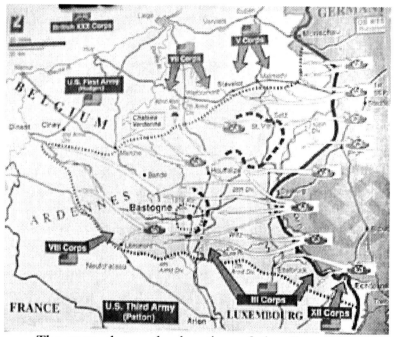

The map shows the location of the German and the American defense lines on December 18, 1944. Dotted line indicates the American defense line at that time.

As we entered the center of Stavelot which was located north of the Ambleve river in our half-track we met up with two American MPs (Military Police). Lt. Willyard stopped and

117

talked with the two MPs and engaged in a conversation with them about various things and especially about baseball. They discussed setting up the best defensive position across the Ambleve river on the south side. The MPs pointed out a likely area across the river and up the hill near the big buildings that was there. The MPs spoke our english language very well and knew all the right answers about baseball that Lt. Willyard asked. They gave us no reason to suspect them. The MPs turned out to be German soldiers dressed up in American uniforms wearing MP bands on their arm.

Lt. Willyard was given orders to take the 2nd platoon, A Company 526 Armored Infantry across the Ambleve river to the south side and there set up a defensive position. We immediately started digging fox-holes in that hard frozen ground to set up our defensive position.

Our Headquarters squad of the 2nd Platoon with Lt. Willyard, S/Sgt Lowe's squad and S/Sgt Crumpton's squad all in our half-tracks crossed over the south side of the Ambleve river. Possibly two half-tracks of the 825 T.D. Battalion also crossed over. As I remember five half-tracks crossing over to the south side of the Ambleve river that morning. After crossing the bridge our half-tracks angled up a road to the left then we stopped by a bunch of two story apartment buildings that were all joined together.

S/Sgt Lowe saw a soldier walking guard up near the buildings on the hillside. He walked up towards the soldier and they both realized here were two enemies facing each other. S/Sgt Lowe recovered his shock that this was a German soldier and immediately shot him.

At this time we discovered we were in the middle of Col. Joshen Peiper's army sleeping quarters. He had over four thousand five hundred soldiers and ninety tanks at his command. Col. Joshen Peiper had with him the 1st and 2nd SS Panzer divisions that were the crack troops of Hitler's army. They were considered the cream of the German army.

We were probably less than fifty soldiers on the south side of the Ambleve river in battle with them that morning. We all knew that we were in the battle of our lives when we encountered that large German army in the early morning at about three A.M. on the 18th of December, 1944.

After this all hell broke loose. I heard later that S/Sgt Lowe was wounded but I don't know if it was then that he was wounded. Lt. Willyard yelled to all of us that were digging fox holes to come back to the halftracks to reform. Bullets were flying all around us then as we were getting to the half-track. Germans were firing out of the second story windows that were all along where the half-tracks were parked at that time. Apparently the Germans had moved into those apartment buildings sometime earlier that night before we got there.

It was at that phase of the battle when Ralph Quesenberry was shot in the stomach. I never knew the out come for Ralph and have not heard since that time.

Lt. Willyard gave orders to go clean out those buildings that the Germans were firing down at our half-tracks. I had reached the second story of the building near where our half-track was parked when I heard Lt. Willyard yell, "let's get the hell out of here." I took those steps two and three at a time to get down to the street level because I could hear the half-track was already pulling out.

Outside on the street I had to run to catch up to the half-track. I grabbed hold of the bedroll carrier that was fastened to the back of the half-track. I crawled up on the bedrolls and fired at the flashes. It was a very dark and cold night.

119

It was easy to determine what guns were making those flashes in the night by the sound of the guns being fired. The German burp guns as we called them had the capabilities to fire six hundred and fifty rounds per minute in short bursts. If they fired their gun continuously it was possible it would burn up the barrel of the gun. We called them Burp guns because the Germans fired them in short bursts.

I continued to fire at the burp flashes. The bullets were flying around so fast and furious it was like a bunch of bees around a beehive. At that time there were so many bullets flying around that the only thought was just staying alive. With all that action going on it didn't give a person time to be afraid. I am sure that on that day God had his protective hand over all of us during all of that activity.

Ambleve river bridge

We came to the bridge that we must cross over to the north side of the Ambleve river. The problem was to get back across the river without getting blown up by A Company Third Platoon 526 Armored Infantry as they were holding defensive position on the north side of the bridge. We traveled fast to get to the north side of the bridge hollering to tell them that we were Americans; to let us through. They must have gotten the message because we traveled right on back without a shot fired from the north side of the river.

Allen Breed A CO.Medic

S/Sgt Lowe's squad got to the bridge when their half-track hit a cable stretched across the road. It disabled their half-track. Sgt Stap removed the firing pin from the fifty caliber machine gun mounted on the half-track before leaving to retreat across the bridge to the north side of the river. Allen Breed CO. Med. half-track picked them up.

S/Sgt Crumpton's machine gun squad was following in their half-track a little distance behind S/Sgt Lowe's half-track. S/Sgt Crompton's squad, in their half-track, came under intensive fire from the Germans. Finally their half-track became disabled.

A grenade wounded PFC John Sankey at that time. Everyone in S/Sgt Crompton's squad dismounted from the half-track and retreated to the bridge. PFC John Sankey was wounded but he continued to retreat with the rest of his squad.

121

At that same time Allen Breed, a 526 armored infantry

PFC John Sankey

medics half-track passed the disabled half-tracks. They slowed down for all the Americans that were retreating on foot to load into their half-track thus giving all of S/Sgt Crumpton's squad a chance to pile in that half-track and all get across the bridge.

On the way back across the bridge PFC John Sankey hung onto the side of the half-track because there was no more room in the half-track. Bullets were flying all around at the half-track that PFC John Sankey was holding onto as they crossed the bridge.

As the half-track came to the north side of the Ambleve river bridge PFC John Sankey decided that with all the bullets flying around it would be better to jump off the half-track and head for the first building. He found a gate near the building that allowed him to move around to the back side. He saw that German soldiers were crossing the bridge. One German soldier followed him around to the back of the building and PFC John Sankey shot him.

I also heard later that S/Sgt Crompton was wounded. I do not know for sure if his wounds came from this battle. Also PFC Bill Lang was wounded but I could not confirm if it was in this battle that he received his wound. I also know that PFC Elmer Reaves was with us at the Chateau Grimonster but I do not remember seeing him after the battle.

The Third Platoon of the 526A.I.B. had set up a defense position on the Stavelot side which was the north side of the bridge with two 57 MM anti tank gun emplacements with S/Sgt Carl Smith and PFC Roscoe Taylor at the control of these guns. The German 88 Tiger tank started to cross the bridge as S/Sgt Smith fired the artillery 57 MM gun at the tiger tank. The shell just bounced off the tiger tank. He shot again hitting the track of the tiger tank and disabling it. The tiger fired at the 57 MM anti tank gun destroying it.

S/Sgt Carl Smith went over to the second 57 MM anti tank gun, aimed and struck the turret of the 88 Tiger tank. In the meantime Lt. Jim Evans and two other soldiers were up the line a short distance. They came to investigate the situation. The 88 tiger tank fired killing Lt. Jim Evans. S/Sgt Jack Ellery of the third platoon went to see what was going on and was also killed there.

At this same defensive location PFC Lloyd Fisher and PFC Dale Nelson were killed. They were also from the third platoon of 526 A.I.B. Staff Sargent Smith and PFC Roscoe Taylor both received the silver and bronze star.

S/Sgt Boyce Williams

At the same time when all of this had been going on Staff Sargent Boyce Williams of the first platoon of A Company had positioned his squad along the Ambleve river on the north side. Many of the German soldiers tried to cross the river. The river was deep enough in places that the Germans had to hold their guns up over their heads. It was no easy task for them to cross that river in zero degree temperature on a very dark night. S/Sgt Williams's able squad stopped them before they could get up onto dry ground again.

Ambleve river foot-bridge

A little further up the line along the north side of the Ambleve river there was a foot bridge that the Germans wanted to secure to quickly get their troops across the river to the north side. From the American defense point of view this footbridge had to be quickly blown. T/Sgt Duesdieker was the platoon sergeant of the first platoon of A Company 526 A.I.B. He volunteered to blow the bridge. Despite constant firing from both sides, T/Sgt Duesdieker went back over to the footbridge four times before the bridge was completely blown. For his bravery under fire to complete this task T/Sgt Duesdieker received the Bronze Star. T/Sgt Duesdieker was temporarily attached to the 30th infantry division at that time. The bridge was 300 yards ahead of the most frontal forward position.

Going back to Headquarters squad with Lt. Willyard after they crossed back over the Ambleve river to the north side with the American defense line we continued into Stavelot. At the city center in Stavelot we met Major Solis, Captain Mitchell and Lt. Oppenhiemer. They were going to reorganize us when we saw those deadly 88 Tiger tanks start to cross over the bridge into Stavelot. The 526 Armored Infantry Battalion did not have any artillery capable of destroying those Tiger tanks.

Major Solis

I think wisdom would dictate to any one that it was time to get the hell out of there. Captain Mitchell told Lt. Willyard we should go to the north side of Stavelot and reform there.

As our half-track headed out of Stavelot we headed for a big gas dump stored in five gallon cans that stretched out as far as you could see. The German tiger tanks spotted us and the race was on. T/5 Jack Stredwick, our

Captain Mitchell

driver, did a super job of driving. The hits from those tiger tanks landed in front of us, back of us and along side of us as T/5 Jack Stredrick weaved that half-track back and forth. Those 88 shells kept landing around us but not close enough to injure any of us.

Finally we turned into a grove of trees to hide from those deadly tanks. After getting into the grove of trees next to the big gas dump Lt. Willyard spread us out parallel to the gas dump and told us to load our guns with tracers. Every third bullet load a tracer. Lt. Willyard ordered us to commence firing. From the result of that command the gas dump went up in flames. We had fired into a pretty big section of that gas dump.

From that big roaring fire we could see those German tanks slow down and stop because their plan to get all of that gas to use was gone. The German Tiger tanks seemed to be confused with what had happened so they turned around and went back down into Stavelot.

PFC Willard Ingraham

I know for sure that the fire that was coming from that gas dump was the biggest fire I had ever seen. The gas dump consisted of army five gallon gas cans piled up at least three high and stacked in sections that left some space between sections. Some say that this dump extended back along the road for seven miles.

There are other claims of setting fire to that gas dump that could be because the gas dump covered a long distance. We lay claim to setting a forward section of the gas dump when we saw those German 88 Tiger tanks coming closer. At that time we saw no fires burning in that big gas dump.

Later when the 117 Infantry came and entered the battle to push the Germans back across the river the fire in the gas dump was snuffed out and left many miles of gas dump still intact.

Later that night when I unrolled my bedroll I counted twenty-three bullet holes in it. Those bullets entered the bed rolls when I was sitting on them and firing at the flashes.

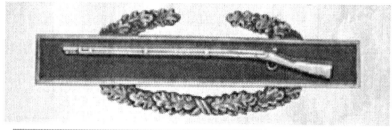

From that earlier morning of our first encounter with the Germans from that battle that day I received the Bronze Star and the Combat Infantry Badge.

Awardee Must See Combat

The CIB is not an award dispensed lightly. *Army Regulation (AR) 672-5-1* clearly outlines the requirements for awarding the CIB. First and foremost, a recipient must have an infantry military occupational specialty (MOS). This includes not only infantry regulars, but also tactical infantry advisors, Rangers, Special Forces and airborne troops with the requisite MOS.

He must also be an infantry officer in the grade of colonel or below, a warrant officer or an enlisted man.

An awardee must satisfactorily perform his duty while assigned or attached to an infantry brigade, regiment, battalion, company or smaller-size unit during any period such unit was engaged in active ground combat. Mere presence in the hostile area or battle participation doesn't always entitle a soldier to a CIB.

Major Solis commanded the First, Second and Third platoons of A company, 526 Armored Infantry, one platoon of 825 tank destroyer battalion and the 202nd Engineers. Also the headquarter company of the 526 armored Infantry Battalion.

It had been planned that bridge crossing the Ambleve river, going into the center of Stavelot, was to be blown by the 202nd Engineers but later Major Solis ordered the engineers to remove the mines from the bridge. The only thing I can say is, "thank God for Major Solis," because if that bridge had been blown while we were over fighting on the south side of the bridge all of us Americans on that side would have been annihilated.

All of us felt sad and sorry for the people of Stavelot that lost their lives when we allowed the Germans back over the bridge to the north side. We had tried our best to hold them but we were highly out numbered and out gunned. The people of Stavelot lost 164 lives that morning when the Germans reentered Stavelot murdering them in a short time.

Is Awarded Badge

Mr. and Mrs. Lyle Ingraham have just received word from their son Willard saying that he and the other members of his group have been awarded the Combat Infantryman badge for actual participation in combat against the enemy in the Belgium front. Standards for the badge are high. The decoration is awarded to the Infantry soldier who has proved his fighting ability in combat. The handsome badge consists of a silver rifle set against a back ground of infantry blue, enclosed in a silver wreath.

Our artillery and bazookas were like pea shooters compared to the 88 German Tiger tanks. The 526 Armored Infantry Battalion was just a thorn in their side compared to the massive German army we tried to hold back that morning.

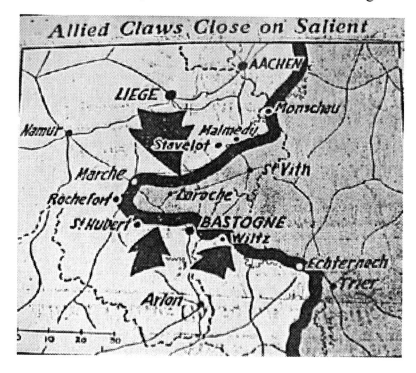

A company of the 526 Armored Infantry lost two half-tracks on the south side of the Ambleve river that day. The 825 T.D. Battalion lost their two vehicles on the south side of the river that day. The 526 Armored Infantry lost many soldiers in our group that day. They were killed or wounded; captured or missing. This battle was known as part of the spearhead of the Battle of the Bulge. Malmedy was also a part of the Belgium Bulge.

131

The defense line at Malmedy needed help so Major Solis sent the First Platoon of the 526 A.I.B. led by Lt Beardsley and the Second Platoon of the 526 A.I.B. led by Lt Willyard to help beef up the defense line at Malmedy, Belgium. This meant, as a part of the 2nd Platoon, I would be going along with Lt. Willyard.

The 117 Infantry Regiment 30th Infantry Division arrived in Stavelot and helped to send the Germans back across the Ambleve river. Major Solis assigned Captain Mitchell with the third Platoon of A Company 526 Armored Infantry and the Headquarters Company of 526 Armored Infantry to remain in Stavelot and help the 117 Infantry Regiment 30th Infantry Division.

One to our Credit Stavelot

On this page you can view a good tiger tank. When I say a good Tiger tank I mean one that has been disabled.

CHAPTER X

MALMEDY

All of us of the 526 A.I.B. had already heard of the massacre that had happened on December 17, 1944 at Baugnez Crossroads. Eighty-six Americans were captured by the Germans and then killed by machine gun, rifles and pistol shots. As we passed by this area on the way to Malmedy and viewed all the bodies strewn around in that field a great anger welled up in all of us. We determined not to give the Germans any quarter in the future. The massacre had taken place the day before we viewed it so the bodies were all out in the open with no snow covering over them.

After arrival into Malmedy our adrenalin was still running on high. We had not had any sleep since the night of the sixteenth of December and our bodies were just running out of steam. We billeted in Malmedy that night with all of us inside a building with cots furnished for sleeping quarters. At this time it seemed like a luxury to us to just get a good nights sleep. I must admit that during the night I did have some of my wildest dreams.

The next morning the first and second platoons of A Company 526 Armored Infantry Battalion set up a defense line

German Tank
Battalion lined up in
battle formation

outside of Malmedy along a railroad track. We were able to repulse any German thrust trying to breach our defense lines with artillery pieces and infantry units spread out down the line.

When the German tanks spread out in battle formation and headed our way across the large open front the artillery went to work leaving many of those tanks to burn. It took some of those burning tanks two days to completely burn out.

The railroad track was built up high enough to give us a very good barrier from small arms fire. It was very cold with a lot of snow on the ground but we soon got used to living out in the open in that harsh winter weather.

Out in front of us about eight hundred yards there was a fairly large house with big broken windows because of the artillery explosions. One evening during the light of the day I saw the Germans move into that house. They tried to cover the open windows with blankets. I thought, by damn if I have to stay out in this cold you are not going to cover those windows to keep warm in the light of this day. I shot at those windows every time they tried putting their blankets up to cover them. It wasn't long they left the blankets down at least until it got too dark outside to see the house through the darkness clear enough to shoot.

After dark we heard those lumbering German tanks coming in with the clicking sound of their tracks. We determined with all the activity on the German line it would probably be an interesting time the next day. Many times it was but the Germans never managed to breach our defense line.

We held our line pretty well but apparently the Ninety Ninth Infantry Battalion was having their problems with the

Germans. The Ninety Ninth Infantry Battalion was on the right of our defensive line. T/Sgt Leonard Landolt was 2nd Platoon A Company 526 A.I.B. platoon sergeant. He asked S/Sgt Clark Moots to go check out what was happening to the Ninety Ninth Infantry Battalion because we had been hearing a lot of gun fire from their location.

S/Sgt Clark Moots

S/Sgt Moots took PFC Henry Little who was from the Headquarters Squad, A Company with him to investigate the statice of the 99 Infantry Battalion. Before they got to the 99th three young soldiers came running towards them in a great deal of fear. One had a bullet hole in his leg. They told S/Sgt Moots that they were all that was left of the 99th. The rest had been killed or captured. Later that was found not to be true.

S/Sgt Moots took his group of five with him and headed back to tell T/Sgt Landholt what he had heard. On the way back he kept telling everyone not to bunch up together because he knew the danger of bunching up in a war zone. As they were nearing a small solid cement building a German artillery shell exploded near S/Sgt Moots breaking his right leg and injuring his right arm. Two of the men from the 99 Infantry Battalion were lying about four feet from him and were both dead. He told PFC Little to get the hell out of there as they might soon fire another shell over their way. He told PFC Little to take the other soldier from the 99th that had the bullet hole in his leg with him and send some one back to help him.

After PFC Little left five or six shells exploded around his area. He tried to crawl up the hill toward the cement house to get into some shelter as he began to get cold. As he crawled his shattered leg prevented him from crawling well dragging that useless leg. The bone was already completely shattered so he thought maybe he could cut his useless leg off. He got his pocket-knife out to cut it off but it cut like tough leather so finally he gave up. He had previously placed his belt on his leg as a tourniquet to stop the flow of bleeding. He sat up and pushed himself backward on up that hill to the cement house. Finally he made it to the house and with a great deal of difficulty he got the door open and finally inside.

S/Sgt Moots had to wait several hours before help came to get him. It took them quite a while to find him because they were unaware that he had crawled up the hill into that cement house. When they opened the door of the house S/Sgt Moots had a grenade in his hand. He told them if the Germans had come to take him he was not going out alone. As S/Sgt Moots was carried past our defense line he gave us the high sign that he would be all right. I would say he was a very brave man. It was something you would expect from a good man like S/Sgt Moots.

He recovered from his wounds minus a leg and lived until June 26, 1984. I remember S/Sgt Clark Moots from the beginning of the 526 A.I.B. in our basic training at Fort Knox, Kentucky. He had an easy going manner and quick laugh that no one could forget. He was an inspiration to all of us young recruits who were just leaving home for the first time in our lives. He served in the Rifle Squad, 2nd Platoon A Company 526 Armored Infantry Battalion from March 20, 1944 to the time of his discharge sometime in 1945.

During the time we were holding our defense along the railroad track outside of Malmedy we observed many days that big groups of B17 and B24 bombers flying overhead on their way to bombing missions some where in Germany. Some days we watched as groups of fifty planes flew over continuously for better than three and a half hours.

B 24 dropping bombs at Malmedy

The Stars and Stripes (an army newspaper written by Erny Pyle) told us that there were thirty five hundred to five thousand planes flying the bombing mission on that particular day of the bombing. We felt pretty good knowing that the Air Force was doing their part in whittling down the strength of Hitler's power.

As I remember, on the 21st day of December, 1944 we looked up and saw a group of B24 bombers flying toward our direction. We made comments like, "There are parts of Germany going to get it today." The bombers were just about over us when to our surprise bombs started dropping on Malmedy, a town that was completely under our control. We thought, "whom in our army could pull a snafu like that?"

The next two days the B24 bombers, some in larger groups came back and bombed Malmedy again. On the third day of bombing we were getting so angry we felt like shooting at the planes. A mistake by someone in the American army had caused an American engineer group and many Malmedy citizens to die. All total, I understand, over three hundred were killed.

A few days prior to the bombing the First and Second Platoon A company 526 A.I.B. had been housed for one night in the same location as the unfortunate engineers. The bombing release was a tragic error.

On the twenty fourth of December we moved away from the railroad track and moved to close the gap toward the 99th Infantry position. We had been in our defensive line position for quite some time and had only one can of C rations per meal. The C can also had a couple of biscuits that were hard as rocks. We could soak them in a hot cup of coffee all day without the biscuit getting any softer. We called them dog biscuits. We did not have any water to drink but there was a lot of snow so we did get our liquids.

From the front position of our defense line we saw the German soldiers walking around their area. Across our defense line there was a small footbridge over a small stream of water. It was about fifteen or twenty feet across the bridge. Some days to make things interesting we ran across that bridge and the Germans immediately fired at us. It became a game betting the Germans could not hit us while we ran across that bridge.

On Christmas day, December 25, 1944 we heard via the grapevine that we were finally going to get a hot meal. It was a turkey dinner to be exact. From our front line position we took turns, in small groups, to go back to the rear C.P. (Control Point) to get our turkey dinner.

It was both, elation and a disappointment when they plopped that black boned piece of turkey on my plate. I was raised on a farm and knew good meat from bad. That turkey was so locker burned that no good cook would have had it in the kitchen but we had been on the C can diet so long that any cooked food tasted better than that.

From eating that meal we suffered because all of the 526 A.I.B. that ate that turkey got dysentery so bad that they had to pull us off the defense line back somewhere to recover for a few days. Can you imagine having that kind of a problem while on the front lines in a fox hole? I guess the good part of it was at least we had nice white snow to clean up with.

I have to go back in time to tell what happened to B Company. Before the battle in Stavelot, B Company 526 A.I.B on December 17, 1944 with L. Col Carlisle Irwin, battalion commander was alerted to prepare for combat. They moved out of their position located at Comblain-La-Tour with in three hours and headed for Malmedy, Belgium.

It was a very cold and dark night and very slow traveling because the drivers of the half-tracks had to drive with their slit lights on the half-tracks. They gave very dim lights to be able to see the road. They were to meet the 99th (Norwegian) Infantry Battalion at Remouchamps, Belgium.

While waiting at Remouchamps one German enemy plane came over and bombed near Remouchamps, Belgium. At 9 O'clock P.M. the 99th Infantry never showed up. The C.O. of T Force then issued orders for B Company 526 A.I.B to go on to Malmedy by way of LaReid, Belgium at once and take A Company 825 T.D. Battalion with them.

While in route to Malmedy one half-track of A Company 825 T.D. Battalion and one half-track of B Company 526 A.I.B pulling a 57 MM A.T. gun temporarily got lost from the convoy. The 99th Infantry Battalion had arrived earlier and the (BTN Co) Battalion commanding officer of the 99th was placed in command and given orders to plan the defense. At Malmedy the 291st Engr. Battalion led the convoy of B Company 526 A.I.B. into town.

B Company 526 A.I.B and A Company 825 T.D. Battalion (less one platoon) were immediately sent out to block all roads leading into Malmedy. B Company Headquarter and Headquarters Company 526 A.I.B were kept in reserve in the town square in Malmedy.

When they entered Malmedy the church bells were chiming the tune, "Yankee Doodle Dandy," which could be heard for miles. The tune was a well recognized World War One tune. The soldiers did not know if some one was trying to warn the Germans outside of Malmedy that the Americans were in their town or if they were welcoming the Americans as they entered Malmedy. The people of Malmedy have confirmed that the tune of "Yankee Doodle Dandy" was played by the church bells and appears in the history of their city.

On the morning of the 18th of December, 1944 Major Solis, commanding officer of both Stavelot and Malmedy operations of battle formations who was T force executive officer informed Headquarters in Malmedy that Stavelot had met strong enemy force and was in desperate need of help. The mortar and assault gun platoons from Headquarters Company 526 A.I.B. were sent to Stavelot.

After being pulled off the front lines because of the dysentery problems right after Christmas of 1944 the 1st and 2nd Platoons of the 526 A.I.B. recovered and were ready to go to work again. We were taken somewhere southeast of Malmedy near Burnenville, Belgium and spread out along another defense line.

One night my squad leader, S/Sgt Gribble called four of us together to brief us on our mission for that night. He said that it was going to be an informational mission to collect all the information we could get from the enemy, the Germans. We were to take no gun, no knives or anything in our pockets. The only thing we were allowed to have were our dog tags around our necks.

S/Sgt Gribble said that the Germans would shoot flares in the air when they mistrusted something might be out in no mans land. Once that flare went up in the air we were not to move, not even if we had one foot in the air for the next step because it was the movement that was easily seen in the night as that flare burned brightly overhead. He told us we would move in a diamond formation with him in the center and each of the four of us would be on a side of the diamond formation.

When we made a turn it would be made in a full ninety degrees with a new leader in front.

We were to be controlled by Gribble, our sergeant, by predetermined clicks to the right, left or reverse direction by him tapping a small stick in his hand. The main thing he told us to remember was not to move when a flare was shot into the air. He told us our forward CP's (the fox hole control point) had been notified that we would be coming back through our defense line later that night. He gave us the password to get back through our own defense check-point. S/Sgt Gribble told us that an important point was if we drew fire from the Germans that one of us must get back to our unit to deliver the information we had gathered on that mission.

We were taken somewhere up the line and dumped off. We were on our own to get back. We moved within a hundred yards of the German camp. They were talking, laughing and it seemed having a good time with their buddies. It was almost like our own American army camp.

We walked very slowly heading back. It was a very cold and dark night and all of a sudden they shot up those flares. Here we were, standing out there in the middle of that open field standing up, not moving a muscle and praying that S/Sgt Gribble was right. We could see their camp very easily so why couldn't they see us? The only thing that happened was the flare only burned bright when shot into the air and quickly disintergrated, then darkness again. Before we got past their camp we went through a lot of the flares with dead stops before we were far enough away to be in the clear. We decided not to stop in and have coffee with them this time.

When we got to the outpost check point for our own front lines it was now to get through that point without getting shot. We had no idea exactly where the check point was but we knew when we got close we would be challenged.

Challenged we were. John West was on duty that night and he was very nervous about letting us through even when he was given the password. Well he should be because when we were so badly fooled with the Germans dressed in American MP uniforms in Stavelot one could not be too careful.

S/Sgt Gribble talked to him for a while until he was absolutely sure we were who we said we were. Until then he would not let any of us move a muscle.

On New Years day, 1945 I watched as a group of American B24 bombers were flying overhead. The German anti-aircraft artillery was not too far forward from our front lines. The anti aircraft shells began to burst around the big bombers. I stood there dumbstruck when I counted fifteen of those bombers getting knocked out of the sky. As I watched I saw quite a few parachute jumpers coming down from the disabled American bombers. I watched in horror as I saw the German small arms fire shoot all of the parachutists out of the sky as they were coming down. I was so mad at that instant in time if a German had walked in front of me I would have shot him on the spot with out any hesitation.

Finally on January 3rd, 1945 Hitler admitted his push to break through the American lines and capture Antwerp, Belgium had failed. There was still a lot of work to be done because the Germans were not pushed back across the Rhine river and back into Germany. The bend in the bulge was still held by the Germans and needed some attention by the American fighting force.

On the morning of the 3rd of January the 1st Platoon of 526 A.I.B. left Burnenville, Belgium. The 3rd Platoon 120

Infantry Division, the 1ˢᵗ Platoon A Co. 526 A.I. B., B Co. Unit from 743ʳᵈ Tank Platoon 823ʳᵈ T.D. Platoon and Mortor Platoon Hdqts Co. 526 A.I.B. all jumped off together on the morning of January 3ʳᵈ for Geromont and preceeded down the road to Baugnez. It was there that they positioned a protecting

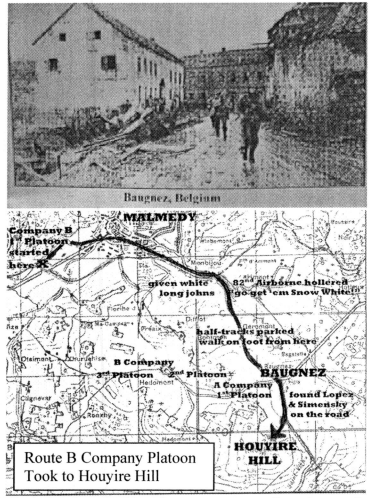

Baugnez, Belgium

Route B Company Platoon Took to Houyire Hill

left flank for the attacking force to act as a diversionary force. This happened near where the Germans, Joshen Peiper, 1ˢᵗ and

2nd SS Panzer division massacred the eighty-six Americans on the 17th of December 1944.

The 1st, 2nd, and 3rd Platoons of B Company 526 A.I.B. 743 Med.Tk Btn and the Mortor Platoon Hdqts 526 A.I.B. was sent for artillery support and would go in as the main force. It was a bitter cold day and snowing lightly. They immediately drew a lot of fire action from the German position. B Company objective was to take Houyire Hill.

B Company 526 A.I.B. started out bunching up too close to each other and immediately suffered many casualties. They took the hill but the fighting force that day all took a terrible casualty loss.

A Company was still holding a defense line somewhere southeast of Malmedy near Burnenville, Belgium. On the night of the 13th of January, 1945 Kenneth Murvine, Cleve Collins and I had duty together on a forward check point about three hundred yards in front of our defense line. We were in a foxhole big enough for all three of us to sit in and be comfortable. We also had with us a phone line that we could keep in touch with the rear C.P. (control Point). I brought along some candles and writing material so I could write a letter home to my parents. For some reason when I started to write, my letter turned out to be a poem. I sent it to my parents and it was published in the home newspaper. My mother kept a copy of the poem as it was published and I have inserted it:

SON WRITES "FOXHOLE" POEM

Mr. And Mrs. Lyle Ingraham received the following letter written January 13, 1945 in rhyme by their son PFC Willard Ingraham, at the fighting front. It gives a glimpse of life in the foxholes and of what the boys "over there" are thinking:

FOXHOLE POEM

As I sit in my fox hole tonight and I think of home
I know for sure I'll never more want to roam
I have a dim light to write this by
As a big light would show into the sky
And with the enemy right over the hill
A big light would give them a chance to kill
I have two buddies now by my side
But this foxhole is big enough for us to hide
One's name is Cleve and the other one Ken
And in my opinion they're both good men
Another buddy, Boyce who is just up the line
Who you know I think of as fine
He was up to my foxhole to see me today
But doesn't come often as he's quite far away
We both send our love from us today
And hope soon to come home and stay
He's a very good buddy who is very true
And helps me out when I'm terribly blue
It's now zero weather and plenty of snow
But we stay on the line and fight the foe
I think of the furlough I so long ago had
But then here's the enemy which makes me so mad
You folks were so good to me when I was home
So over here I feel quite alone
Your letter I receive with lots of cheer
And to me none other can be so dear
I hear from Lorraine, Norman and Ray
But it's your letters Mom that I get most every day
The Yakima valley is the best place to be
But it's far from England with all it's tea
France and Belgium are farther away yet
But you go where you're taken and take what you get
So with this little fox hole poem
You know dear folks I'm thinking of home
By: Willard Ingraham

146

We could have candle light in our fox hole by covering

S/Sgt Boyce Williams

Pfc Kenneth Murvine
I don't have a picture of
buddy Pfc Cleve Collins

with a blanket. I had my harmonica with me so decided that it was time to be a broadcasting station from our front line forward check point foxhole. While I played the harmonica the other two sang. At the same time we opened the circuit of our phone to the rear C.P. so they could hear everything we sang. We called ourselves Ingraham, Murvine and Collins broadcasting company. We did not sing too loudly so that the German enemy could hear and give them an opportunity to kill. Our foxhole was located out in the middle of no mans land.

The 526 Armored Infantry Battalion soldiers were recognized for their battle activities. The ones referred to are the battles of the Belgium Bulge at Stavelot and Malmedy. The fierce

ANOTHER FOXHOLE POEM BY: WILLARD

```
I LIE HERE THINKING
AS THE TIME GOES BY.
HOW THIS WAR IS MAKING
A LOT OF MEN DIE

WAR IS NO FUN
AS YOU ALL KNOW
BUT IT'S GOT TO BE DONE
SO WERE ON THE GO.

WE GO THROUGH CITIES
NOW LAYING IN RUBBLE
IT'S REALLY A PITY
BUT THEY GIVE US NO TROUBLE
```

Written Jan. 1945

fighting against superior German enemy forces occurred in December 1944 and January 1945. From these battles the 526 A.I.B. gained the nickname "Battleaxe." The 526 A.I.B. was authorized to add the word Battleaxe to their 526 Armored Infantry Battalion shoulder patch.

According to 12th Army group, Volume IX, the Battle of Houyire Hill on January 3rd, 1945 cost the 526 Armored Infantry 65 casualties. Nineteen soldiers were killed and eighteen were missing. During the combat of Malmedy and Stavelot casualties were 33 killed, 58 wounded and 24 missing.

I am sure that most veterans of World War II will tell you that the close fellowship that developed among their buddies. When in training together and sharing all the personal daily feelings there was a closeness that developed in each and every one around. It would have been no problem in times of need that one would willingly lay down ones own life for anyone in our organization if the need arose to warrant such a choice and you knew your buddies would do the same.

> **A letter that Willard wrote to his parents while in a foxhole**

Jan 8, 1945
Somewhere in a fox hole

Dearest mother & dad.

I don't know whether this is the right date or not because one day is like another here.

It is a hell of a long ways from being fun.

Right now I'm sitting in a fox hole with Jerry right over the hill. The snow is about two feet deep and it is still snowing. It is tough but one consolation we have and that is that them damn Krauts are going through the same thing only worse for there getting a lot throwed at them now.

They have a lot that they throw back at us to – but brother, I wouldn't want to be in there position now.

They pull quite a few surprise
punches but every time they
do they get it back double!
A guy don't know what they
aim to do next.

Us boys up here have no
more idea of when there going
to fold up - then what you
fellows back home do.

Maybe not as much as we
make the news where every
body back there hears it.

One thing we do know and that
is that were coming in on
the home run now and it is
only a question of time before

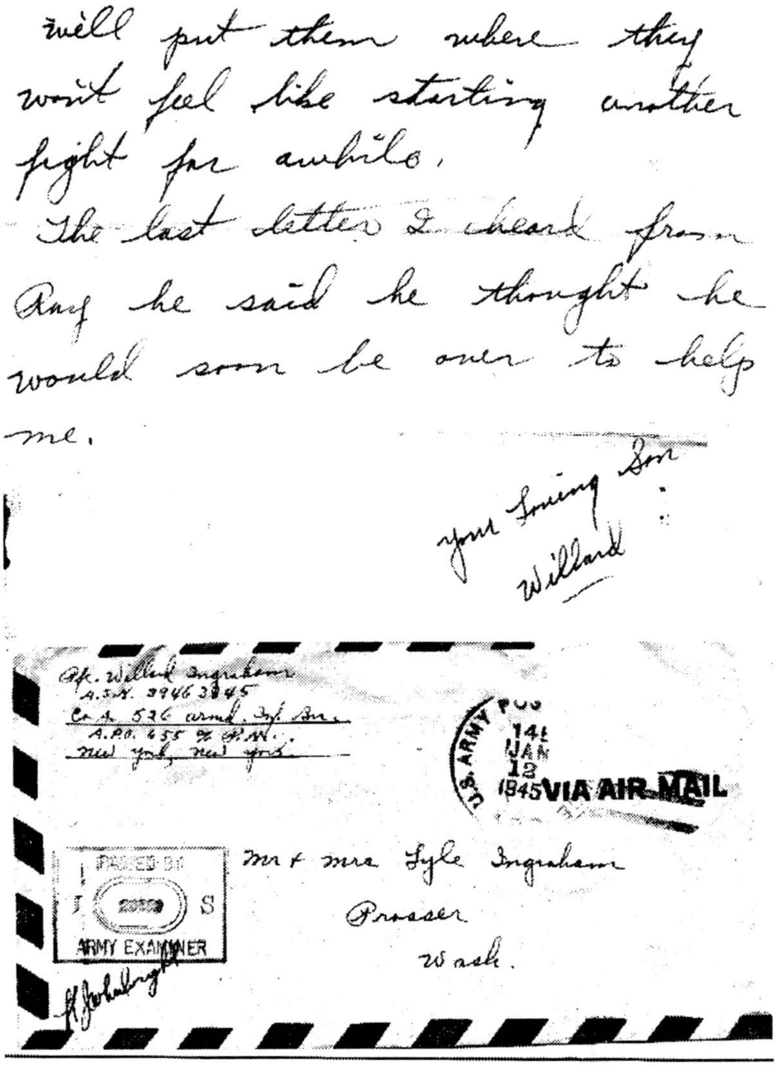

will put them where they
won't feel like starting another
fight for awhile.

The last letter I heard from
Ray he said he thought he
would soon be over to help
me.

your loving Son
Willard

Pfc. Willard Ingraham
A.S.N. 39463845
Co A 526 armd Inf Bn.
A.P.O. 655 % P.M.
New York, New York

U.S. ARMY P.O.
14t
JAN
13
1945 VIA AIR MAIL

PASSED BY
ARMY EXAMINER

Mr & Mrs Lyle Ingraham
Prosser
Wash.

One thing we learned was that when up front in the foxhole in that cold snowy weather we always left a live round in the chamber of our guns. Actually there were two reasons.

One was that we were always ready to fire at any instant of time when needed. The second good reason was that in the cold it was possible for the mechanism of our guns to freeze up. If frozen and we tried to inject a round in the chamber of our guns we were in trouble. If we had a shell already in the chamber of our guns the first shot broke it loose ready for any action after that.

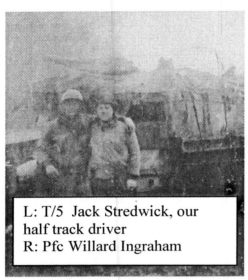

L: T/5 Jack Stredwick, our half track driver
R: Pfc Willard Ingraham

There were times that we were up in that cold snow for thirty days at a time. Some soldiers experienced their feet having been frozen for so long that their feet were turning black. Word was sent down for all of us to take off our shoes when we could and check our feet and if our feet were turning blue or black to rub them as often as time permitted. We were on the defense line at that time. When I checked my feet they were turning blue and I had little feeling. I kept taking my shoes off and rubbing my feet whenever I could and the feeling in my feet slowly returned to normal. There were times up front that we never took our clothes off for a month at a time. Our feet were always cold and we had no idea what was happening to our feet.

The battalion minus C Company had been on the front lines for 31 days and it was time to get them out of the fox holes and off the C can meals.

CHAPTER XI:
T FORCE ASSIGNMENTS

On the 17th of January the 526 Armored Infantry Battalion was relieved from the first U.S. Army and ordered to duty with T Force. Beginning from that time until the first week of March the battalion was engaged in training at Marneffe, Belgium preparing for a mission with T Force. On the 2nd of March the battalion was ordered to move to Eschweiler, Germany.

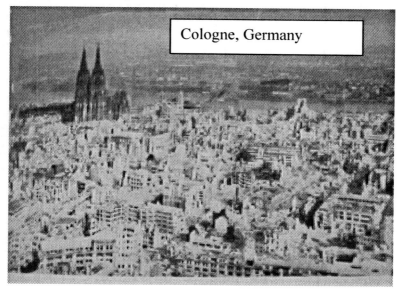

Cologne, Germany

On the 6th of March 1945 the 526 Armored Infantry Battalion entered the city of Cologne and immediately began operations and seizing targets that were of intelligence value. At that time Cologne was the largest city in Germany with a population of 750,000.

The T Force commenced operations according to phase lines agreed upon with Tactical Commander and advanced as the tactical situation permitted. The city was completely open until the afternoon of the 8th of March. The main German army had crossed over the Rhine river east of Cologne.

Cologne, Germany after bombing

As we were the first troops entering Cologne after the American bombing we guarded selected targets to keep them from further damage. We guarded the Cologne cathedral which stood in the middle of all the bombed out buildings. The cathedral was not damaged except for some broken windows. I stood guard protecting that cathedral for several nights to protect it from damage from vandalism.

There was a large building that must have been a hotel that had an outside door to the basement that we entered and found a wine cellar that was a block long. It was filled with rows of bottled wines, champagnes and various other kinds of drinks like cognac all stored in place on shelves.

We found some pink champagne that was dated back to the eighteen hundreds. That champagne was the smoothest and best tasting drink I have ever experienced and probably ever will. We took a few boxes of those great drinks with us and stored them in our halftrack in case we ever got thirsty sometime in the future. Wouldn't you know it; the MPs came into Cologne in a few days and put a seal on that basement wine door.

T Force had entered the city with a carefully selected list of 246 buildings that were targeted and uncovered. In the coarse of operations 39 additional targets of opportunity action on 201 personality targets were completed.

Between the 6th of March and the 13th of March the force involved in the operation totaled 973 persons and 175 motor driven vehicles. An additional 215 investigators representing 24 different intelligence agencies were processed by T Force operations.

That operation furnished the first outstanding example of the value of T Force activities to military government in the use of information gathered incidentally to the T Force mission regarding a wide variety of political, military and industrial installations.

A Company 526 A.I.B. stayed in a partially bombed house while in Cologne. I was searching the house that some of us were staying in and discovered a trap door to the attic of the house. I soon searched out the area and found what was up in that attic crawl space. I found a huge bundle of 5000 mark bills and some in lesser amounts all in one package.

We were told that the German money was no longer any good so we used the 5000 mark bills to light our cigarettes. I don't know what happened to all that money but it soon disappeared.

On the morning of the 21st of March 1945 the first and 2nd platoon A Company 526 A.I.B. was told

L. to R: PFC Nick Manda, T/5 Jack Strewick

that we had to pack up and go to the Remagen bridge to help keep the bridge from being blown up. We took off all loaded in our half-tracks including our boxes of cognac and pink champagne. We got to Bonn, Germany after dark that night all happy as could be because we sampled those

Parked for the night at Bonn

drinks all the way that day.

All the half-tracks pulled into a big open field and parked the half-tracks for the night. After parking we dismounted from the half-tracks and were given our orders for the night. It seemed that I could walk a straight line the best so I was given the job of guard duty along with others that were selected. It wasn't so bad because we were only given four hour shifts.

Pfc Willard Ingraham & halftrack

All of us just unrolled our bedrolls on the ground next to the half-tracks and that is where we slept that night between our shift. The next morning we were up early and left the Bonn area headed for the Remagen bridge. We arrived at the Remagen bridge in late afternoon on the 22nd of March 1945. We found the Remagen bridge was already down in the river.

157

Apparently the American army was so surprised when

they got to the Remagen bridge and found it to be intact that they immediately started to run their army of vehicles across the bridge where they wanted to go. The process was going great for them until the bridge collapsed and trapped 400 vehicles on the bridge.

S/Sgt Boyce Williams

Remagen pontoon bridge across Rhine

By the time we arrived at the Remagen bridge the army engineers had installed a pontoon bridge across the Rhine river to replace the Remagen bridge. It wasn't a long wait before the 1st and 2nd platoon 526 A.I.B. crossed the newly constructed pontoon bridge and were on the east side of the Rhine river for the first time.

A Company was initially responsible for opening up targets in Remscheid, Rummenahl, Dahl, Hagen, Solingen, Schwelm and Gevelsberg, Germany. On the 19th of April with

Dusseldorf, Germany opening up part of A Company along with the anti-tank platoon B Company moved in. B Company then took over part of A Company's targets as well as targets in Barmen, Elberfeld, Langenberg, Velbert, Solingen, Herbedi and Iserlohn, Germany.

When A Company stayed at Dusseldorf, Germany we stayed at a huge concrete room one story below the ground with ceilings about twenty feet in height. There were two more levels of underground with huge rooms under the one we were sacked out in. I did not have to stand guard while we were there.

The street 526 A.I.B. was billeted in Weisbaden

On the 4th of May, 1945 all T Force operations were completed and 526 A.I.B. was released from T Force and ordered to report to Wiesbaden for new duties. T/Sgt Alfred Duesdecker was now our A Company first sergeant.

The move to Wiesbaden, Germany was on the 4th of May with the battalion arriving in the early afternoon after a 125 mile trip. From orders from Duesldorf, Germany the battalion had been given the mission of guard duty in the city of Wiesbaden and vicinity.

159

This territory was divided into zones with each company responsible for a zone including A Company 825 T.D. Battalion then attached.

We were now reattached to General Omar Bradley's 12th Army Headquarters Command now located in Wiesbaden, Germany. He wanted an experienced front line unit to guard Weisbaden because of the German soldiers being released back into civilian life again. He felt confident that the 526 A.I.B. could deal with them because of our guard experience that had been developed in our training. We held many important guard posts in Weisbaden including General Bradley's Headquarter 12th Army group.

I was standing guard in the center of Weisbaden on the night of the 7th of May 1945 when all of a sudden people were hollering and shouting. They were gathered in the street and coming my way. The people mostly Americans were coming out with their bathrobes on to join the group. At that time there were no cellular phones or any way to communicate to my headquarters. I was on my own to handle this large crowd which to me at this time looked like a riot. As they approached down the street I moved out to the center of the street with my gun at port arms to confront them as they came.

I ordered them to halt. They were all laughing and shouting so loud that I had to again shout my order to halt. The long line of people did stop in front of me and asked me hadn't I heard, "the war is over; we mean no harm. We are just so happy that the war is now over."

I could see no harm in this type of celebration so I told them to march on but give me no problem. The surrender came on the 7th of May 1945 but officially it is celebrated as being on the 8th of May 1945. We were all very happy that the

European war was over but we all knew that there was still Japan that had to be dealt with.

On the 3rd of June 1945 with the dissolving of Eagle TAC the C Company 526 A.I.B duties with that echelon came to an end. C Company departed from Bad Wildungen and returned to the 526 Armored Infantry Battalion at Weisbaden, Germany.

A Company 825 T.D. Battalion was released from their attachment to the 526 Armored Infantry Battalion and C Company 526 A.I.B. took over their zone thereby supplementing the 526 Guard. For the first time in eight months the 526 Armored Infantry Battalion was again intact.

From the office, Chief of Military History, SS USA Organizational history and honors branch that they recorded throughout the Battle of the Bulge the 526 Armored Infantry Battalion lost 387 enlisted men and one officer. As a symbol of their part in that bitter fight the colors carry a streamer embroidered Ardennes-Als-Ace.Nor. It is the only symbol retained to commemorate this. It was the units first and hardest fight.

There is in addition a chevron on the distinctive insignia that represents the line so gallantly held at Malmedy. Also on the insignia are three ancient bugles borrowed from the coat of arms of the Provience of Liege where the town of Malmedy is located.

Due to the fact that the after action reports of the 526 Armored Infantry Battalion for the period from the end of the

Belgium Bulge Battle to the close of the war are nowhere to be found. It is not possible to present an adequate account of the combat during the last six month of conflict. Somewhere along the way the 526 became known as the Battle Axes.

Statement of service reads on the inserted document: 526 Armored Infantry Battalion activated 20th of March 1943 at Fort Knox, Kentucky. Inactivated the 25th of November 1945 in Weisbadan, Germany. Activated the 1st of August 1946 at Fort Knox, Kentucky and inactivated the 12th of April 1948 at Fort Knox, Kentucky. A Company activated the

526th ARMORED INFANTRY BATTALION

RA
(Non-div)

Lineage

Constituted in Army of United States 26 February 1943 as 526th Armored Infantry Battalion. Activated 20 March 1943 at Fort Knox. Ky. Inactivated 25 November 1945 in European Theater. Activated 1 August 1946 at Fort Knox, Ky. Inactivated 12 April 1948 at Fort Knox. (Company A activated 2 June 1948 at Fort Knox.)

Campaign Streamers

World War II
  Northern France
  Rhineland

World War II—Continued
  Ardennes-Alsace
  Central Europe

Decorations

Cited in the Order of the Day, Belg Army, for the ARDENNES. (DA GO 43, 1950)

Coat of Arms

Shield. Azure, a chevron, between in chief a battle-ax fesswise and in base three bugle horns stringed, all argent.
Crest. None.
Motto. Validi Milites (Valiant Warriors).
The chevron is used to represent the line held at Malmedy, Belgium, in World War II. The 526th Infantry Battalion, on its first combat mission, was the first combat force to reach Malmedy. The three bugle horns are taken from the coat of arms of the province of Liege in Belgium, where the town of Malmedy is located. The battle-ax, an ancient Infantry weapon, alludes to the organization's nickname.

2nd of June 1948 at Fort Knox, Kentucky and activated (less A Co.) the 10th of April 1954 at Fort Knox, Kentucky. Inactivated the 23rd of September 1957 at Fort Knox, Kentucky.

Campaign participation credit; World War II, Northern France, Rhineland, Ardennes – Alsace and Central Europe. Cited in the order of the day of the Belgium army for action in the Ardennes

T/5 Arnold Steffens

Around the 18th of June I found out that my cousin T/5 Arnold Steffens was at that time stationed at Dusseldorf,

Germany only about 125 miles from Weisbaden. I immediately obtained a pass to go see him. I did not have time to write him a letter to tell him I was coming so I just walked out to the main road to Dusseldorf and put my trusting thumb out. I immediately got a ride with a big eighteen-wheel trucker. It was no problem because the highway was full of mostly American vehicles.

I asked the trucker if by any chance he was headed for Dusseldorf and he told me that matter of fact he was going right through there. When we arrived I asked the trucker if he happened to know of the 2072 QM Trucking Company and he said that he did know of that trucking unit and pointed out the street he thought that I might find them if the trucking unit was still there. As he dropped me off he told me that if I would go straight up the street for about two miles I would locate them if they were still there.

R toL: Pfc Willard Ingraham and T/5 Arnold Steffens

It was a nice day so it did not take me long to cover that distance. As I walked up the street I saw a soldier sitting on a wall about two foot tall along a driveway that was probably two hundred feet off the street. He was guarding the entrance into that complex center and as the trucks entered his area he had a little German boy about nine years old open and shut a wire across the driveway to control any entrance in or out. As I got closer I could not believe my luck as the soldier sitting on that wall guarding the entrance was no other than my cousin that I had come to see.

When I walked up the driveway I asked him how did he manage to let that little boy do all of his work. It had been two years since we had last seen each other but he immediately recognized me and we had a joyous greeting.

Pfc Ingraham and T/5 Steffens

Arnold and I are cousins and only one-week difference in our ages. His birthday is on the 16th of June and mine is on the 23rd of June. It was the 18th of June when I saw him in Dusseldorf . His birthday had passed and mine was coming up. We decided right then and there that we would celebrate our 21st birthday together.

Lt. Litman and Arnold had a friendly relationship so when the lieutenant found out where we were stationed his comment was, "no problem as I have a business engagement in Weisbaden to take care of and it would be no inconvenience for both of you to jump in the jeep tomorrow and I will take you to Weisbaden." I thought how lucky can we be.

The next day with a sergeant as a driver and Lieutenant Litman next to him and Arnold and I in the back of the jeep we took off for Weisbaden. By the time we got to my street and went to my room it was just about time to get into the chow line. I told Lt. Litman that I would introduce him to my officers so he could eat with them and he insisted he would rather eat with us. I told him that would be no problem and rounded up some extra mess kits.

I told him again that our officers most likely would want to meet him but he shrugged his shoulders and again said no. He was wearing an army field jacket rolled up at the collar on his neck to cover his lieutenant bars. Up and off to the chow line we went.

Boyce Williams and I had a big room with two double beds and a veranda built up off the street. It was maybe three feet above the street and just off our room was a table and chairs out on a small patio that had a covered roof and was very private. Boyce and I brought our meals back there everyday.

Willard and Boyce: chow

That evening we began to celebrate Arnold and my 21st birthday and what a memorable time we had. It was getting late and I started to think about how we were going to accommodate our extra three guests then Lt. Litman said no that they had to get back yet tonight. Arnold was in no shape to be going anywhere right then. We decided to sober him up. I probably wasn't in any better shape than Arnold was in but we decided to work on Arnold.

We had a big bath tub in that place so I ran that tub about three quarters full of cold water, undressed Arnold and threw him into that tub of cold water. You should have heard him holler and cuss us out while we were all laughing. It probably wasn't easy on Arnold but I will tell you when we got him up and out of that tub and got him dressed again he was most likely the most sober one of any of us.

After all of this we went back to my room and had another drink. Arnold and I told all of them how much we enjoyed having them all take part in our memorable 21st birthday celebration in Weisbaden, Germany on that June day 1945.

The next day the officers heard that I had an officer as a guest and they asked me why I didn't tell them. I didn't figure I owed them an explanation so I said nothing. They told me the next time an officer comes into our company they wanted to know about it. Yes sir, I told them.

We did have good officers in our 526 unit so we were willing and able to follow through on commands that were given to us. We were also taught to use our own initiatives and think on our own at those times that were necessary. The men were all exceptional and it was an honor to have served with so many brave and trustworthy soldiers.

I am very proud of the 526 Armored Infantry Battalion and all the soldiers I served with knowing that we all did make a difference in fighting for peace in World War II.

Willard and Boyce
On the Rhine

Willard

Boyce Williams and I decided to get a pass to take a boat ride down the Rhine river in Germany. Now that the war

Boyce

was over on the European continent it was much easier to do things like that. We could now also get a pass to go to different places now and then. We still had our work to do serving the 12th Army Group under General Omar Bradley doing the guarding of Wiesbaden. The MPs (military police) were now there so we served in guarding General Bradleys headquarters specific governmental buildings and industrial buildings and so forth. It was enough to keep all of us quite busy everyday.

Headquarters
Twelfth Army Group

Europe

Pfc Willard S. Ingraham, 39463345

I need not speak of your past accomplishments, other than to say you have reflected great credit upon yourself and your command.

We are now fighting on German soil, and we are in contact not only with the soldiers of our enemy but also civilians of Germany. As conquerors, we must now consider our relations with the people of Germany.

It is imperative that you do not allow yourself to become friendly with Germans, but at the same time you must not persecute them. American soldiers can and have beaten German soldiers on the field of battle. It is equally important that you complete the victory over Nazi ideas.

To guide you I have issued these special "battle" orders. They may appear to lead along a narrow path, but they are NECESSARY. You personally must prove to the German people that their acceptance of Nazi leadership is responsible for their defeat, and that it has earned for them the distrust of the rest of the world.

O N Bradley

LIEUTENANT GENERAL, U. S. ARMY
COMMANDING

Somewhere in Dusseldorf, Germany I acquired a German accordion that I probably drove some wild, with practicing tunes I had heard. I do not play by note, only by ear as the tune sounds to me so at times it may not be the same as if it were played by note.

Willard & accordion

I wish I had paid more attention to the cars the people in Europe ran around in. They were powered by attaching a small stove like container on the back of the car. They put coal or wood or whatever would burn in that cylinder like stove and built a fire in it. They piped, I would imagine hot water into the motor someway and it drove like any car. This type of contraption was attached to many different makes of cars so it must have worked on any that they installed this make over on.

This is a car that had a fire pot on the back to heat the water.

We had two places we could go for entertainment while in Weisbaden.

169

A company Buck Down Club was one that we could go get our favorite bar drink while we sat around and shot the bull; slang for we would gather and fellowship together.

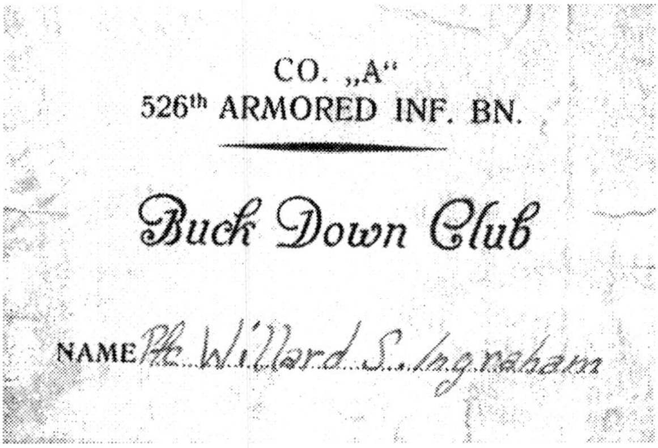

CO. „A"
526th ARMORED INF. BN.

Buck Down Club

NAME *Pfc Willard S. Ingraham*

There was another place of entertainment we went to that was called the Blue Room where there was a large dance floor with many tables and chairs set up around the dance floor. There was good music played by a live band that was capable of playing most of the popular dance songs of America. George Wendt played with this band many times and they gave us really good music to dance to.

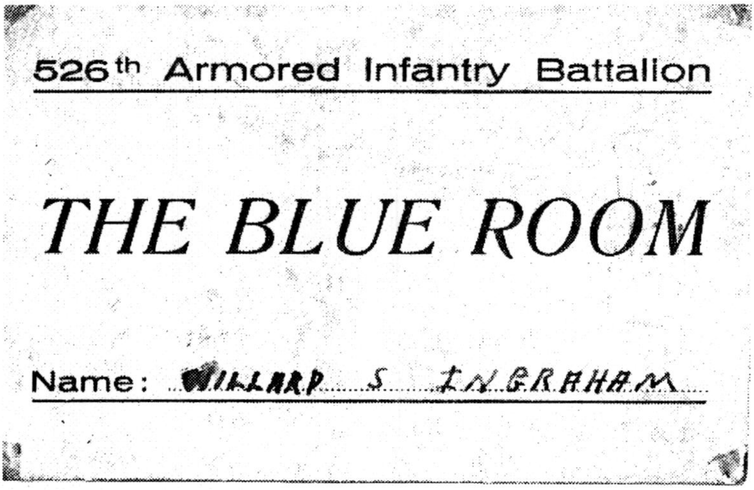

526th Armored Infantry Battalion

THE BLUE ROOM

Name: *WILLARD S INGRAHAM*

170

There was still a lot of guard duty to do and practice street formations and a little marching so we would not get too rusty and forget our marching commands. S/Sgt Williams and I would get out and practice rifle judo now and then. Inserted pictures show us in practice before I had to go on guard duty.

A CO. sign

We had a sign for A Company installed as we entered into the A Company area. We did not mind the duty here at Weisbaden because we had very good lodging with good hot meals every meal and three times a day.

The war in Japan was still raging on in August of 1945 and we began to hear rumors of what was going to happen to the 526 A.I.B. next concerning being sent to help finish the war in Japan. Word was we would be sent home then given a thirty day furlough and off to Japan we would go.

The next thing we heard was that the Boeing B-29 Superfortress Enola Gay with a couple of other planes had dropped a super bomb called an atomic bomb on a couple of cities in Japan and completely destroyed those cities. The Japanese shook their heads in disbelief and immediately surrendered.

The documents of surrender were signed on the Big Mo, the battleship Missouri that was anchored in Tokyo Bay on the 2nd of September 1945 by the Allied powers and the Japanese. The greatest war in history ended on that day of the signing.

A picture of the Enola Gay is shown on its return from that bombing mission that was to end all wars. Now that the war was completely over, our thoughts returned to the fact that now we would be going home soon to stay.

We then heard of the point system that they were using to figure out when we would be elgible to return home. It was so many points for a soldier with a family, so many points for

172

being married, so many points for time over seas, so many points for combat and then it was considered the rank you held.

L to R: Pfc Bill Rogers, S/sgt Boyce Williams & Pfc Willard Ingraham

Some started to leave soon after that. The rest of us stayed for a while. I guess they were not too happy to release us from guard duty yet.

I am going to include some pictures of our company that were taken after many were already on their way home. I give Pfc Norm Phihaly much credit for his foresight in taking and gathering pictures and publishing a book of the history of A Company 526 Armored Infantry Battalion. It preserved some of the history of our great unit in World War II that would have otherwise been lost forever.

Pfc Willard Ingraham

The following section is devoted to photos of those who served in the CO. A 526th Armored Infantry Battalion.

526 A.I.B. Commander
Lt. Col. Carlisle B. Irwin

A Company Commander
Capt. Charles Mitchell

Front: Row-John F. Kalisek-Perry W. Dykes-Dennis M. Callahan-Victor Prohaska-Anthony Bruno-Joseph Giammona-Chris Bruninger-Richard W. Cautcrucin-Marvin P. Orvic

Second: Row-George F. Robertson-Louis Belezzueli-Ollie Murray-Charles Candeau-Earnest P. Garcia-Louis Leyva-Albert C. Hill-Joseph A. Carroll

Third: Row-Ralph J. Gadagno-Harvey S. Shirrmacher-Robert Earl-Kenneth Murnine-Jacob A. Zigler-Marvin Edwards-Russel R. Fears-Albert Pope-Alvin L. Fosbrink-Joseph B. Tibbs-Everett M. Perterson

Front: Row-Junior B. Woodson-William Rogers-Boyce Williams-Willard Ingraham-Robert Harman-Henry Oas-Bernard Tuskin-Patrick Tiedeman-Charles F. Thompson

Second: Row-Albert Duisdecker-Robert Murphy-R. Mackin-Robert Smothers-George F. Irvine-Hersal V. Jacobson-Joseph Graupmann-William Hunter-William Hensleigh-Frank R. Vaga

Third: Row-Earnest Washmuth-Robert Walters-Herman Saxon-Russel Garcia-Reed Tucker-Mario Estrada-John Sitnik-Paul Cabri-John Mills-Robert G. Floyd-Carl Honaker

Front: Row-Keith E. Howe-Milton Johnson-Michael Sorrentino-L. James Pladzke-James P. Bishop-Chas. P. Nabers-Karl A. Kasner-Marcus Wright-James Fields.

Second: Row-Kelly Cornett-Nicolas Manda-John Gribble-Clyde Miller-Vincent Testa-James Farnsworth-Benjamin Day-Joseph Chacon-Ernest Kennedy-Bige Eversole.

Third: Row-William J. Kenny-William J. Heuer-Norm. C. Pihaly-William Liccn-Harold Baker-Standy D. Hammack-Chas. L. Sheets-Charles D. Reed-John West-Frederick Manska

COMPANY "A"
626TH ARMORED INFANTRY BATTALION
(ON 18 DEC. 1944)

Commanding Officer   Capt   MITCHELL, Charles A.
Executive Officer   (?)   (?) See NOTE

HQ PLATOON

PltLdr (?)   (?)   See NOTE

HQ SECTION

SecLdr	(?)	(?)	SeeNOTE
FirstSgt	1st/Sgt	LOWRY, William A.	
CoClk	Sgt	CUSHING, Elmer H., Jr.	
Radioman	Sgt	TIEDEMAN, Patrick J.	
HT Driver	T/5	(?)	
?	(?)	(?)	
	(?)	(?)	
	(?)	(?)	
	(?)	(?)	
	(?)	(?)	
	(?)	(?)	

ADMINISTRATIVE, MESS AND SUPPLY SECTION

Sec Ldr	(?)	(?)	See NOTE
2Sgt Driver	(?)	(?)	
2Sgt Driver	(?)	(/)	

ADMINISTRATIVE UNIT

Mail Clk	T/5	THOMPSON, Charles F.
MT Driver	Pfc	CORDOVA, William R.
	Pfc	JACOBSON, Hersal V.
	Pfc	SCHOTTLANDER, Heinz

MESS UNIT

MessSgt	S/Sgt	MORRISON, Junior B.
Cook	T/4	BAILY, Euis J.
Cook	T/4	NAYLOR, James
	(?)	(?)
	(?)	(?)
	(?)	(?)
	(?)	(?)

MAINTENANCE SECTION

Maint O	(?)	(?)	See NOTE
MaintSgt	S/Sgt	BELL, Robert A.	
HT Driver	T/5	IVEY, Wallace A.	
MT Driver	(?)	(?)	
Mech	T/5	BELLEZINUI, Louis	
Mech	T/5	MISFELDT, Dayton W.	
Mech	(?)	NELSON, Dale B.	
Mech	(?)	MARTIN, Dave	
Armorer	T/5	ERSKINE, Charles W.	
	(?)	(?)	

SUPPLY UNIT

SupSgt	S/Sgt	POCIASK, Bruce
SupClk	T/5	(?) LANE, Charles
SupClk	T/5	(?) CANDAU, Charles J.

NOTE: This is strictly a Jerry rigged organizational and manning chart and, except for the functional headings, may bear little, if any, resemblance to the official Table of Distribution (TD) SORRY!!! Other than the C.O. and the combat platoon leaders two or three other officers were authorized slots in the company. Two of them were 1/Lt Louis J. OPPENHEIMER and 2/Lt James WHEELWRIGHT. The third may have been a 2/Lt LARSON. The senior Lieutenant may have filled the C.O.'s Executive Officer slot and also a Section Leader slot (if such slots were authorized). Instead of the XO filling two slots one of the other officers may have filled two of the Section Leader slots. Records indicate there was a Maintenance Officer slot. But not knowing what other officer slots, if any, existed in the platoon a knowledgeable person and/or a TD would be required to determine these officer slots and, hopefully, which officers filled them.

1ST PLATOON, COMPANY "A"
526TH ARMORED INFANTRY BATTALION
(ON 18 DEC. 1944)

Page 2

11-32

Platoon Leader - 2/Lt BEARDSLEE, Charles F.
Platoon Sergeant- T/Sgt BURSDICKER, Alfred V.

HQ SQUAD

Sqd Ldr	S/Sgt	WILLIAMS, Doyce L.
MT Driver	T/5	KATZ, Solomon
	Pfc	BITTINGER, Harlan A.
	Pfc	DORN, Samuel J.
	Pfc	DARIEN, William R.
	Pfc	HOWE, Keith C.
	Pfc	MILLS, John G.
	Pvt	REDZOWICZ, Fred
	Pfc	SCHNEIDER, Irwin R.
	Pfc	SIPNIK, John W.
	Pfc	WASHBURN, Ernest L.

2D RIFLE SQUAD

Sqd Ldr	S/Sgt	BELL, James F.
Asst Sqd Ldr	Sgt	MOATS, Clark
MT Driver	T/5	(?)MURRAY, Ollice J.
	Pvt	CASA, Dante B.
	Pvt	BEDO, Francis G.
	Pvt	ESTRADA, Mario
	Pvt	FISHER, Lloyd
	Pvt	GARCIA, Ernest P.
	Pfc	LEGG, James R.
	Pfc	MUSCAB, Frank
	Pvt	SCHIPRILITI, Rosario F.
	(?)	(?)

1ST RIFLE SQUAD

Sqd Ldr	S/Sgt	HARMON, Robert L.
Asst Sqd Ldr	Sgt	BREININGER, Christian
MT Driver	T/5	ENFIELBING, Thomas L.
	Pvt	CURTIS, (?)
	Pfc	DEXTER, William A.
	Pfc	MATA, Milario M.
	Pfc	MURCHY, Robert F.
	Pfc	OLSON, Clarence F., Jr.
	Pfc	POLLARD, Barry A.
	Pfc	SAXON, Norman F.
	Pfc	SHAW, Robert E.
	Pfc	SMITH, Raymond E.

MACHINE GUN SQUAD

Sqd Ldr	S/Sgt	BRENNAN, Edward V.
Asst Sqd Ldr	Sgt	MILLARD, Leland
MT Driver	T/5	BRENNAN, John P.
	Pfc	BENDER, Clarence J.
	Pvt	BLASS, Frank
	Pfc	MERRILL, Oscar B.
	Pfc	CAVALLARO, Savino G.
	Pfc	GALLIMAY, Lee M.
	Pfc	GARCIA, Russell J.
	Pvt	BORINOWITZ, Henry
	Pfc	BUSCHEK, Ralph R., Jr.
	Pvt	STEWART, Albert W.

MORTAR SQUAD

Sqd Ldr	S/Sgt	IRVINE, George K.
MT Driver	T/5	GIARDONA, Joseph F.
	Pfc	COCHRANE, Kenneth K.
	Pfc	HENSLEIGH, William R.
	Pvt	MC KENZIE, Frank
	Pfc	MONTROSS, Lawrence L.
	Pfc	OAS, Henry J.
	Pfc	SMITHERS, Robert L.
	Pvt	WALTERS, Robert L.
	(?)	

← 3rd name

```
                    COMPANY "A"
           526TH ARMORED INFANTRY BATTALION        Page 3
                  ON 18, DEC.1944
```

COMMANDING OFFICER: CAPT MITCHELL, CHARLES A.-9465217

33

2ND PLATOON

Platoon leader   1/lt   WILLYARD, Harry L. - 01307600
Platoon Sergeant T/Sgt   LANDOLT, Leonard   -36079025

HQ SQUAD

S/Sgt	GRIBBLE, John L.		MACHINE GUN SQUAD
T5	STREDWICK, John R.	S/SGT	LOWE, Dewey M.
PFC	INGRAHAM, Willard S.	SGT	STAPP, Jerome V.
PFC	COLLINS, Cleveland	T/5	OSBORN, Daniel M.
PFC	MACHEM, Greve B.	PVT	CAUTERUCIO, Richard W.
PFC	MANDA, Nick	PFC	HENDRICKSON, Edward D.
PFC	ROBERTSON, George	PFC	LANG, William J.
PFC	McCAMPBELL, Eugene	PFC	McCARRELL, Henry O.
PFC	KASPER, Ludvik	PFC	ORVIK, Marvin P.
PFC	LITTLE, Henry T.	PFC	ROMANOFF, Julius

1ST SQUAD

MORTAR SQUAD

S/SGT	DYKES, Raymond R.		
T/5	IVEY, Wallace	S/SGT	CRUMPTON, Charles H.
PFC	MURVINE, Kenneth	T/5	DYKES, Perry W.
PFC	PANDORA, James	PVT	CLARK, Larry
PFC	HAMMACK, Stanley	PFC	KALISEK, John F.
PFC	THOMPSON, Jerry	PVT	PROCHASKA, Victor
PFC	ZIEGLER, Jacob	PVT	RAMSDELL, Robert W.
PFC	FIELDS, James	PFC	ROGERS, William A.
PFC	HILL, Albert C.	PVT	SANKEY, John
PFC	PEPE, Albert T.		

2ND SQUAD

S/SGT	WRIGHT, Marcus
T/5	FLOYD, Robert G.
PFC	JOHNSON, Robert W.
PFC	MOYER, Walter
PFC	SCHEIDT, Howard
PFC	CALLAHAN, Victor
PFC	QUESENBERRY, Ralph
PFC	SHEETS, Chas
PFC	WOODBURN, Paul E.
PFC	ROTH, Sam
PFC	BRUNINGER, Richard

3D PLATOON, COMPANY "A
326TH ARMORED INFANTRY BATTALION
(ON 18 DEC. 1944)

Platoon Leader   - 2/Lt EVANS, James J. (KIA 18Dec44)
                     2/Lt WHEELWRIGHT, James J. (Replaced Lt Evans
                                                    18Dec44)
Platoon Sergeant - T/Sgt MANSKA, Frederick S.

HQ SQUAD

SqdLdr	S/Sgt	CURRAN, Gordon G.
HT Driver	T/5	FEARS, Russell H.
	Pfc	DAY, Benjamin F.
	Pvt	DELBRIDGE, Raymond C.
	Pfc	ROMERES, Prudencio R.
	Pfc	SHEETS, Charles L.
	Pfc	TIBBS, Joe B.
	Pvt	VEER, Vernon E.
	(?)	(?)
	(?)	(?)
	(?)	(?)

2D RIFLE SQUAD

SqdLdr	S/Sgt	HEUER, William J.
AsstSqdLdr	Sgt	PARKHURST, Elmer E.
HT Driver	T/5	CROSSWHITE, Leslie L.
	Pfc	HILOTTI, Anthony J.
	Pfc	EAM, Robert V.
	Pvt	FENNELL, Glen L.
	Pfc	MELLO, Rudolph
	Pfc	MILLER, Clyde W.
	Pfc	RODRIGUES, Edward P.
	Pfc	RUH, Joseph P.
	Pvt	WOLF, Morris A.
	(?)	

1ST RIFLE SQUAD

SqdLdr	S/Sgt	HUBBLE, Clarence H.
AsstSqdLdr	Sgt	ST. MICHEL, Maurice K.
HT Driver	T/5	EDWARDS, Marvin
	Pfc	CURTIS, Joe L.
	Pfc	FIELDS, James A.
	Pfc	FOSSMINK, Alvin L.
	Pfc	GASIOR, Joseph F.
	Pfc	GRAUEMAN, Joseph M.
	Pfc	KISER, William I.
	Pfc	MARTINEZ, Juan F.
	Pvt	THOMPSON, James E.
	Pvt	WARFORD, Owen H.

MACHINE GUN SQUAD

SqdLdr	S/Sgt	ELLERY, Jack W.
AsstSqdLdr	Sgt	BARNES, Herbert D.
HT Driver	T/5	FAINSWORTH, Hugh J.
	Pfc	ARCHAMBAULT, Phillip N.
	Pfc	BARTLETT, Edward R.
	Pfc	CORNETT, Kelly
	Pfc	KENNY, William J.
	Pfc	LANDGREN, James
	Pfc	FINALY, Norman F.
	Pfc	SCHIRRMACHER, Harvey S.
	Pfc	TESTA, Vincent F.
	Pfc	TISBRO, Charles

MORTAR SQUAD

SqdLdr	S/Sgt	JOHNSON, Milton R.
HT Driver	T/5	HABAKER, Carl S.
	Pfc	HENZEL, Donald T.
	Pfc	JIMINEZ, Miguel
	Pfc	JONES, Fontain M.
	Pfc	MOODY, Earl
	Pfc	SORRENTINO, Michael P.
	Pfc	VEGA, Frank R.
	(?)	(?)
	(?)	(?)

179

Last Roll Call

Men of the 526th Armored Infantry Battalion WW 11
who gave their lives in service to our country

Headquarters Company

Donald D. Hauger
Harry J. Moyles
Robert R. Sullivan

"A" Company

Harland E. Bittinger
Jack W. Ellery
James J. Evans
Lloyd E. Fisher
Dale B. Nelson
Ralph Quisenberry

"B" Company

Donald J. Banks
Gordon L. Blaisdell
Warren H. Blankenship
Hugo G. Brossmann
Dallas W. Buchanan
Harry E. Burile
John C. Bush
Sam Colosi

James C. Coslett
Robert E. Craven
Leo J. Day
William C. Duncan
William D. Ferguson
Joe G. Ferina
David J. Heron

John A. Hess
James L. Higgins
Donald E. Hollenbeck
Ralph L. Iverson
Delbert J. Johnson
Warren H. Knoelke
Rosco Lively

John M. Lopez
Oliver L. Love
Ralph G. Manis
Lillard B. McCollum
Moises A. Moreno
Ralph C. Russell
Warner Schuster
Francis L. Snyder

Medical Detachment

Joseph A. Ricks

IN REMEMBRANCE
This Remembrance list names men who were members of the 628th Armored Infantry Battalion.
KIA denotes men who were killed in action. DIS denotes men who died in service. Names that
are not marked are men who became deceased after the war.
May these BRAVE and HONORABLE men rest in peace.   * new additions

The transition of the German soldiers back into civilian life went very well for the most part. There were times that we had to pull them back in line. The Air Force personnel that were fresh from the states were really afraid to walk down the street.

One night I was walking back to my quarters from being at the Blue Room and this air force soldier quickly caught up to me and asked if I would mind if he walked with me. He said that he was fresh from the states and walking down those sidewalks at night scared him to death.

We began to notice that some of the Germans started to take advantage of that fear. The Germans walked down the middle of the sidewalk and made the air force soldiers walk out in the street to get by them then the Germans would laugh. They thought it was great to show their superiority. We were aware of what was happening and were on the watch for such an occurrence.

181

One night one of our soldiers in A Company 526 A.I.B. caught two big Germans doing that with an air force soldier. He walked up to the Germans and told them that he had observed what they had done and ordered the Germans to get off the street. The Germans reply was that they did not have to because they had passes that allowed them to be there. The A Company soldier then asked to see their passes. Upon getting the passes he tore the passes up in small pieces and ordered the Germans off the street. The Germans immediately picked up the pieces of their passes from the ground and took off because they knew they were now in great trouble without those passes.

Normally when The Germans observed our shoulder patch on our uniform they never messed around with us. The civilian people as a whole were very friendly and cooperative.

It was October of 1945 and many of our group had already filtered out to go home. After Captain Mitchell left Lt. Marcus Kasner came in to control the rest of us.

CHAPTER XII
GOING HOME

We were alerted one morning to get packed and told that we were all going home. The halftracks were brought up to our street in Weisbaden where we had been billeted since the 4th of May 1945.

Arrival at railroad track

After we loaded up we were on our way to the railroad station. We had no idea what type of train we would be riding in until we arrived at the station. The halftracks stopped and we

Loading up in cattlecars

unloaded along some railroad tracks and the halftracks left. That was the last time we saw those halftracks.

After a while a freight train pulled up and stopped with a bunch of cattle cars attached. We did not pay much attention to them until Lt. Kasner told us to load up that this was our transportation to Antwerp, Belgium. It was cold out but not bitter cold. We thought what the heck because we were now on our way home and didn't care about the kind of transportation.

Our one night stay in quanset houses

We got to Antwerp and lodged in some quanset houses overnight. The next morning we loaded up on a liberty ship called the S/S Irwin MacDowel. We left Antwerp, Belgium on the 6th of December 1945.

Willard Ingraham at quanset house

The liberty ships were ships that the U.S.A. put together in mass production just for WWII for that purpose. About half way across the ocean we hit a terrible storm. The captain sealed all the metal doors to the deck for three days.

Before they sealed the doors up I had an opportunity to peek outside on the deck. I saw that water was washing across the deck as the ship dipped down slapping the ship at that instant making the ship shudder. As the ship dipped down a forty-foot wave the ship would raise to the peak of the wave causing the propeller of the ship to come out of the water and spin like crazy. This action continually repeated the same performance.

Bill Rogers aboard ship on the way home

When we saw the sailors were all afraid we asked why. We felt they should be used to those kinds of waves during an ocean storm. There reply to us was, "Do you know what kind of ship you are traveling on? These ships were mass produced and have been known to split in two in weather like this."

Most of us soldiers thought what the heck we are on the ship and there is nothing we can do about it so at this point we are all along for the ride. After fifteen long days we entered the harbor in Boston, Massachusetts. On arrival I quickly sent a telegram to my parents telling them of my safe arrival.

ARMY SERVICE FORCES

TRANSPORTATION CORPS

ARMY OF THE UNITED STATES

NEW YORK PORT OF EMBARKATION

Pfc Willard S Ingraham 39463345

returned to the UNITED STATES on the
ship s/s Irvin MacDowell
which sailed from Antwerp to Boston
on 6 Dec 1945

Sig George W Pace, Lt Col.
Title Transportation Corps
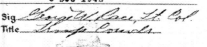

We debarked from the ship in single file with our duffle bag. I was also carrying an accordion I had brought with me. On our walk to get into a building to wait for our train the Red Cross met us with a pint of milk for each of us. That was the first milk we had tasted in two years so to us it was an enormous treat.

In the waiting room they had a small box about nine inches square that we could watch moving pictures on. They called it a T.V. We had no idea it existed. We were told that within ten years the T.V. would be in most homes in America. We just shook our heads and said someone must be dreaming. I must tell you that they were wrong. In 1954 I bought our first T.V. and that was four years less than the ten year prediction.

We left Boston on the train headed for Chicago, Illinois where we had a transfer of trains. I had relatives in Chicago so called my aunt Edna Anklam. She told me that my cousin, Harriet Anklam and her would try to make it down to the railroad station to see me. I had only an hour for transfer and they had a long way to go in that Chicago traffic to get there.

In the mean time Lt. Kasner had arranged a meal for all of us at the station while we waited for our train. Edna and Harriet Anklam did make it to the station in time. It was a joyous meeting even though the meeting was short. It was a very memorable time catching up on news.

L to R: Harriet & Edna Anklam

I had another uncle and aunt Otto and Esther Warnke living in Chicago. They had two sons in the army and lost one son, Marvin Warnke, in battle in

Marvin Warnke

Memorial for: Marvin Warnke

France shortly after he was sent to the European theatre in 1944.

Soon we were aboard in sleeper cars on the train headed out of Chicago and headed for the west coast to Fort Lewis,

Washington. It was a five day ride on the train. We spent Christmas day of 1945 traveling on that train. The holiday meal on the train was nothing special but we didn't care as we were just about home again.

ENLISTED MAN'S TEMPORARY PASS

Ingraham, Willard S   Pfc   39463345
(Name)   (Grade)   (Army serial No.)

CO C WDPC FT LEWIS WN
(Organization)   (Station)

is authorized to be absent—

From 0900 Dec 27, 45 To 1200 Dec 28, 45

To visit Tacoma

Signed HOWARD E ORVIS
CAPT. C.E.
W. D., A. G. O. Form No. 7
28 June 1943
Commanding Officer.
(OVER)
*This form supersedes W. D., A. G. O. Form No. 7, 8 September 1942, which may be used until existing stocks are exhausted.

Finally we arrived at Fort Lewis that was located close to Tacoma, Washington. It took us three days to prepare for mustering out of the army. Wallace Ivey was also in the 526 Armored Infantry Battalion and was mustering out of the army the same time as I did. He lived in Tacoma so one night while we were at Fort Lewis we got a pass to go to Tacoma. He had asked me to go along with him. I gladly accepted. I don't know where he got his car but he already had a car and showed us the lights of Tacoma that night.

The night of the 29th of December 1945 I was discharged from the army and proudly wore my ruptured duck discharge emblem. I boarded a train from Fort Lewis that was headed for Prosser, Washington.

I got into Prosser about one o'clock A.M. on the 30th of December 1945. I left my army duffle bag and my accordion that I had brought back from Germany at the train station. I walked down town in Prosser to the only business, Riches Café that was open at that time of night to see if by chance this town had a taxi. It was no such luck. I thought perhaps someone I would know would come into Riches Café but again no luck.

My parents, Lyle and Gena Ingraham lived on their farm four miles from town. Walking wasn't a problem for me. I probably ran half the distance to get there that night.

My parents had just gotten home shortly before I got there. They had been out playing music for a dance that night. My father was an old time fiddle player and my mother played the piano. After waking them up and having a most joyous home greeting my father wanted to go back to town to pick up my duffle bag and accordion yet that night.

I had left my things on a bench at the train station. Everything was there. Thinking about it I bet I would not have anything to pick up if I left it on a railroad station bench today.

Mother went on to bed when we got home but Dad wanted to talk to me some more so we talked the rest of the night through until morning.

It was the 30th of December 1945 and the first thing I did upon returning home and getting adjusted

Pfc Willard Ingraham to private citizen

to civilian life again was to go into Prosser to a photographer studio. I had my picture taken while I was still wearing my uniform. Then I had another picture taken to see what I looked like in civilian clothes.

L to R: Willard and brothers and sister Norman, Lorraine and Raymond 2002

My cousin, Arnold Steffens returned from service one month prior to my coming home. Robert Ingraham, my cousin and my two brothers, Raymond and Norman Ingraham all returned home to Prosser, Washington in 1946.

All of us found our wonderful life soul mates and raised families with successful and happy lives. Norman Ingraham married Verdell Noble Ingraham. Raymond Ingraham married Anna Crosby Ingraham. Both couples have now celebrated their 50th wedding anniversary.

Arnold Steffens and I found two beautiful

Verdell and Norman Ingraham

190

Anna and Raymond
Ingraham   2004

and wonderful sisters who became our soul mates. We had a double wedding on September 13, 1947. Arnold married Lucille Williams Steffens and I, Willard Ingraham, married Louise Williams Ingraham.

From our marriage Louise and I had two daughters. Mahria Carol and Mary Ann. In later years Mahria married and gave us three grandsons, Jon Rosson, Paul Jordan and James Jordan. Mary Ann married Milton (Joe) Hicks. From that union we have a granddaughter, Shannon Hicks.

In 1997 Arnold and Lucille Steffens and I, Willard, and Louise Ingraham all celebrated our 50th wedding anniversary together with all of our families.

In 1998 we were all saddened when Arnold passed away. My parents, Gena and Lyle Ingraham passed away in the 1980s.

Lucille and Arnold Steffens
1992

We are fortunate that my two brothers and wifes, Norman and Verdell Ingraham and Raymond and Anna

191

Ingraham, and sister Lorraine Johnston all live within twenty miles of each other. We often get together to play cards and to socialize.

I have devoted this page and the next page to my own family and to my grandchildren. They are the pride of all my years and the most important thing in my life. When I was a boy on the farm in N. Dakota I dreamed of having my own family one day and I have

Willard & Louise Ingraham
2003

Mahria Jordan

Mary Ann & Milton Hicks

never been disappointed in the hand that God has dealt me. As one grows older we have more time to contemplate and to think

192

Jon Rosson

James Jordan

Shannon Hicks, Air Nat. Guard

Paul Jordan

how our lives have been enriched. First in my life was my wife, Louise, and then our daughters, Mahria and Mary Ann and later our son-in-law Milton and then the grandchildren. I proudly pass down to the next generation all the qualities each of them have to offer others.

526th Memorial, Armor Memorial Park, Ft. Knox

Camp Bouse

CAMP BOUSE
THE 526TH A.I.B.
CANAL DEFENSE LIGHT PROJECT
DESERT TRAINING CENTER
CALIFORNIA-ARIZONA MANEUVER AREA

CAMP BOUSE WAS ESTABLISHED IN BUTLER VALLEY 30 MILES BEHIND THIS MONUMENT IN SEPT. OF 1943. IT WAS ONE OF TWELVE SUCH CAMPS BUILT IN THE SOUTHWESTERN DESERTS TO HARDEN AND TRAIN UNITED STATES TROOPS FOR SERVICE ON THE BATTLEFIELDS OF WORLD WAR 11. THE DESERT TRAINING CENTER WAS A SIMULATED THEATER OF OPERATIONS THAT INCLUDED PORTIONS OF CALIFORNIA AND ARIZONA. THE OTHER CAMPS WERE YOUNG, COXCOMB, GRANITE, IRON MOUNTAIN, IBIS, CLIPPER, PILOT, KNOB, LAGUNA, HORN, RYDER AND RICE.

CAMP BOUSE WAS THE HOME OF THE 9TH TANK GROUP WHICH CONSISTED OF SIX TANK BATTALIONS, ONE ARMORED INFANTRY BATTALION, AN ORDNANCE COMPANY AND A STATION HOSPITAL. THE GROUP TRAINED IN ABSOLUTE SECRECY MAINLY AT NIGHT. THE LIGHT DEVICE CONSISTED OF A HIGH POWERED SEARCH LIGHT, MOUNTED IN AN ARMORED HOUSING ON A TANK. ITS PURPOSE WAS TO TEMORARILY BLIND THE ENEMY AT NIGHT. THE ROLE OF THE 526TH INFANTRY WAS TO DEFEND THE OPERATION OF THE CD TANKS AND ATTACK IF SECURITY OF THE TANKS WAS BEING THREATENED.

.THE 526TH AIB WAS SEPARATED FROM THE 9TH TANK GROUP IN FRANCE, AUGUST 1944 AND WAS ASSIGNED TO THE 12TH ARMY GROUP HDQS UNDER COMMAND OF GEN. OMAR BRADLEY. "C" COMPANY BECAME A SECURITY UNIT FOR GEN BRADLEY IN LUXEMBOURG. THE REMAINDER OF THE BATTALION WAS HEAVILY INVOLVED DURING THE BATTLE OF THE BULGE, FIGHTING THE ENEMY IN THE BELGIAN TOWNS OF TROIS-PONTS, STAVELOT, MALMEDY, HEDOMONT, BOUGNEE, AND GEROMONT.

AFTER THE BULGE AND UNTIL VE DAY THE 526TH BECAME PART OF "T" FORCE. THE PURPOSE OF "T" FORCE MISSIONS WERE TO SEIZE, SAFEGUARD AND PROCESS ENEMY DOCUMENTS, ARCHIVES AND MATERIAL OF INTELLIGENCE OR COUNTER-INTELLIGENCE AND CAPTURE ENEMY AGENTS, MILITARY OFFICERS AND KEY COLLABORATORS.

THIS MONUMENT IS DEDICATED TO ALL THE SOLDIERS THAT SERVED HERE AND ESPECIALLY FOR THOSE WHO GAVE THEIR LIVES IN BATTLE, ENDING THE HOLOCAUST 7 DEFEATING THE ARMED FORCES OF NAZI GERMANY.

PLAQUE PLACED BY THE LOST DUTCHMAN, BILLY HOLCOMB, JOHN P. SQUIBOB CHAPTERS, OF THE ANCIENT 7 HONORABLE ORDER OF E CLAMPUS VITUS, THE 526TH ARMORED INFANTRY BATTALION ASSOC AND IN CO-OPERATION WITH THE BOUSE CHAMBER OF COMMERCE.

There are memorials placed at Fort Knox, Kentucky, Bouse, Arizona, Chateau De Grimonster, Belgium, Stavelot,

Belgium and Malmedy, Belgium. They are in honor of the 526 Armored Infantry Battalion to commemorate and mark the time in history that the 526 A.I.B. passed through these places to serve their part to win the peace in the battle for freedom in WWII.

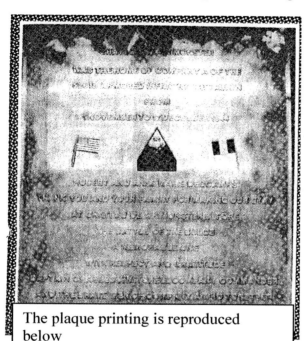

The plaque printing is reproduced below

CHATEAU DE GRIMONSTER

was the home of Company "A" of the
526th Armored Infantry Battalion
from
1 November to 17 December 1944.
Hubert and Anne-Marie Descamps,
"Thank you" and your family for making our stay
at Chateau de Grimonster before
The Battle of the Bulge
a memorable one.
With respect and gratitude,
Captain Charles A. Mitchell, Company
Commander and the brave men of "A" Company
who together
we served.

The city of Stavelot, Belgium has a plaque in the city center square and one of A Company's 526 Armored Infantry Battalion half-tracks in their memorial park. They are in honor of A Company 526 A.I.B. when we fought there in December of 1944.

Allen Breed on the Rhine River

526ᵗʰ A.I.B. CHAPLAIN MESSAGE
by Allen Breed ~ Medical Detachment~
e-mail: beachcombrr@earthlink.net

A SYMBOL OF OUR LIVES

Did you know that at military funerals, the 21-gun salute stands for the sum of the numbers in the year 1776?

Have you noticed the honor guard pays meticulous attention to correctly folding the American flag 13 times? You probably thought it was to symbolize the original 13 colonies, but we learn something new everyday!

FOLD 1 – The symbol of life.

FOLD 2 – Symbol of our belief in eternal life.

FOLD 3 – In honor and remembrance of veterans departing our ranks.

FOLD 4 – Represents our weaker nature, for as American citizens trusting in God, it is to Him we turn in peace and war.

FOLD 5 – A tribute to our country.

FOLD 6 – This fold is for where our hearts lie. It is with our hearts that we pledge allegiance to the flag.

FOLD 7 – A tribute to our Armed Forces.

FOLD 8 – In tribute to the one who entered into the valley of the shadow of death, that we might see the light of day.

FOLD 9 – A tribute to womanhood and Mothers, whose faith, love, loyalty and devotion has molded us to make this country great.

FOLD 10 – A tribute to Fathers who have given sons and daughters for the defense of our country.

FOLD 11 – Represents the lower portion of the seal of King David and King Solomon glorifying, in Hebrew eyes, the God of Abraham, Isaac and Jacob.

FOLD 12 – Represents the Trinity.

FOLD 13 – The 13 fold or when the flag is completely folded, the stars are uppermost reminding us of our nation's motto, "In God We Trust".

After the flag is completely folded, it takes the appearance of a cocked hat, ever reminding us of the soldiers who served under General George Washington, and sailor and marines who served under Captain John Paul Jones, who were followed by their comrades and shipmates in the Armed Forces of the United States, preserving for us the rights, privileges and freedoms we enjoy today.

I thought it would be most appropriate to add this symbol of our lives sent into the Pekan newsletter by Allen Breed. I remember Allen when we served in the A Company 526 Armored Infantry Battalion.

I leave my story for your own interpretations. The memories that I have are indelible in my mind. Many of the photos are my own. There are other photos and illustrations presented that would not have been possible without the generosity of others.

ORDER FORM:

FARM BOY TO SOLDIER
WORLD WAR II
AUTHOR: WILLARD INGRAHAM
PUBLISHED BY:
BIZY ENTERPRISES, INC.
929 N. VAL VISTA DRIVE
SUITE 107 #191
GILBERT, AZ. 85234

WEB ORDERING: WWW. MINDSEYEVISION.COM
OR
MAIL ORDER:

Each Book $21.95: Quanity:_____Total $_____
Shipping & Handling:
U.S. $4.95 for first book---------------------$_____
$2.95 for each additional book----------- $_____
7.8% Sales Tax for Arizona addresses---$_____
     SUB TOTAL $_____
International shipping:
$10.00 first book
$5.00 each additional book
    TOTAL AMOUNT:-------------------- $_____
    ENCLOSE CHECK OR MONEY ORDER

MAIL TO:

NAME:_____
STREET:_____
CITY:_____STATE_____
ZIP:_____
E-MAIL: _____
SEE WEB SITE FOR OTHER BOOK OFFERINGS:
WWW. MINDSEYEVISION.COM

Printed in the United States
41541LVS00003B/102

9 780972 262118